BEHOLD (THEN SINGS MY SOUL)	4
LOVE SO GREAT	15
LOOK TO THE SON	28
CROWNS	40
WHAT A BEAUTIFUL NAME	51
YOUR WORD	63
LET THERE BE LIGHT	75
IN CONTROL	89
GRACE TO GRACE	99
ELOHIM	113
I WILL BOAST IN CHRIST	122
AS IT IS (IN HEAVEN)	133

HILLSONG WORSHIP
Our Hillsong Worship album is the combined effort of our Hillsong Church worship teams to express both our personal devotion and a congregational offering of worship. Ever-committed to resourcing individuals, worship teams and churches alike, the Hillsong Worship team seeks to bring songs that are as diverse as the greater Church herself is. Our prayer each year is that our Hillsong Worship album would offer songs for all generations and demographics that are declarations of faith and adoration.

UNITED AND Y&F TEAMS
UNITED is committed to writing songs that speak truth, create a unique sound, connect with churches, individuals and ultimately connect people everywhere with God. Young & Free (Y&F) is the creative worship expression of Hillsong Church's current youth movement. Both the UNITED and Y&F teams serve in church as a part of the wider Hillsong Worship and Creative team when they are home. When on tour, they are accompanied by the whole Hillsong team's support and prayers that their ministry would arrest hearts and point people to Jesus, impacting individuals, local youth groups and local churches.

WE ARE A CHURCH COMMITTED TO INSPIRING AND EMPOWERING THE AUTHENTIC WORSHIP OF JESUS AND RESOURCING THE BODY OF CHRIST.
There are numerous resources we as Hillsong make available including inspiring teaching and books by Brian & Bobbie Houston, curriculum content that can impact your children's, outreach and discipleship ministries, and of course music. For more information visit hillsongmusic.com

WE ARE A CHURCH THAT BELIEVES IN CHAMPIONING THE CAUSE OF THE LOCAL CHURCH.
Hillsong Conference is about you, your church and seeing God's Kingdom advance across the earth. This is your chance to lean in, receive and take home practical teachings you can outwork in your own church home, family and community. It's about being refreshed and inspired and finding great strength and unity amongst the diversity of the local church worldwide. For more information visit hillsongconference.com

WE ARE A CHURCH THAT BELIEVES IN PLACING VALUE UPON WOMANHOOD.
Colour Conference, at the very core is a strong humanitarian message. Our passion and labour is to place value upon womanhood, so that we in turn can arise from a place of strength and cohesion and place value upon fellow humanity. For more information visit colourconference.com

WE ARE A CHURCH THAT BELIEVES IN REACHING AND INFLUENCING THE WORLD WITH THE MESSAGE OF JESUS CHRIST.
Hillsong Channel is an innovative media movement, beaming the timeless message of JESUS around the globe into television screens and digital devices to empower people in every sphere of life. This is a platform positioned in the heart of culture bringing JESUS into prisons and palaces all over the world. For more information visit hillsongchannel.com

Hillsong Television with Brian Houston is a half-hour Christian television program that features his teaching from Hillsong Church services. Pastor Brian's messages are empowering, passionate and practical for everyday life. His teaching will inspire you with the hope, joy, meaning and purpose that can be found in a personal and loving God. For more information visit hillsongtv.com

WE ARE A CHURCH THAT BELIEVES IN PARTNERSHIP AND UNITY AS WE ADVANCE HIS KINGDOM ON EARTH.
The Hillsong Leadership Network is all about connecting, equipping and serving leaders, and exists to champion the cause of local churches everywhere. Our heart is that by coming alongside leaders, churches and ministries of varying denominations and styles, we are able to see more churches flourish and reach their God-given potential through this membership program. For more information visit hillsong.com/network

WE ARE A CHURCH THAT BELIEVES IN EQUIPPING PEOPLE WITH PRINCIPLES AND TOOLS TO LEAD AND IMPACT IN EVERY SPHERE OF LIFE.

To find further information about the Pastoral Leadership Streams (including Youth, Children, Event Management, or Social Justice Pathways), Creative Streams (including Worship Music, TV & Media, Dance, or Production) or a Degree Program offered on campus by Alphacrucis College visit hillsongcollege.com

WE ARE A CHURCH IN MANY LOCATIONS...
Australia, UK, Kiev, South Africa, New York City, France, Stockholm, Germany, Amsterdam, Copenhagen, Barcelona, Los Angeles, Moscow, Buenos Aires, São Paulo, Phoenix. For service times and information visit hillsong.com

TERMS AND CONDITIONS
Thank you for purchasing sheet music from Hillsong Music. Your purchase grants you the right to make ONE copy of the sheet music for your personal purposes (performances, worship services, personal study, musical teaching, etc). However the following rights have NOT been granted to you:
1. Reproduce copies of the sheet music in whole or in part outside of the rights granted to you above.
2. To translate, enhance, modify, alter or adapt the sheet music or any part of it for any purpose.
3. Cause or permit any third party to translate, enhance, modify, alter or adapt the sheet music or any part of it for any purpose.
4. Sub-licence, lease, lend, sell, rent, distribute or grant others any rights, or provide copies of the sheet music to others. Reproductions of the sheet music can be made for the purpose of church worship only with an existing Music Reproduction Licence from CCLI. For further information contact CCLI at http://www.ccli.com

For further information about copyright or other use of this music, please contact Hillsong Music Publishing at publishing@hillsong.com

TRANSCRIBED & ENGRAVED BY JARED HASCHEK

BEHOLD (THEN SINGS MY SOUL)

BEHOLD (THEN SINGS MY SOUL)

Words & Music by Joel Houston

VERSE 1:
Behold the Father's heart
The mystery He lavishes on us
As deep cries out to deep
Oh how desperately He wants us
The things of earth stand next to him
Like a candle to the sun
Unfailing Father
What compares to His Great love

VERSE 2:
Behold His holy Son
The Lion and the Lamb given to us
The Word became a man
That my soul should know its Saviour
Forsaken for the sake of all mankind
Salvation is in His blood
Jesus Messiah
The righteous died for love
It wasn't over
For He is the risen One

© 2016 Hillsong Music Publishing.
All rights reserved. International copyright secured.
Used by permission.
Tel: +61 2 8853 5300
Email: publishing@hillsong.com
CCLI Song No. 7068430
Inspired by "How Great Thou Art!", courtesy of The Stuart Hine Trust

CHORUS:
Then sings my soul
Then sings my soul
How great Your Love is
How great Your Love is

VERSE 3:
Behold I have a friend
The Spirit breathing holy fire within
My ever present help
Speaking truth when I can't find it
Light up this broken heart and light my way
Until my time on earth is done
Oh Holy Spirit
Breathe in me like kingdom come
Oh Holy Spirit
Let Your work in me be done

OUTRO:
Then sings my soul my God
He who was and is to come
Prepare the way
Until the work on earth is done

Watch as the clouds He rides swing low
Lift up the sound
As He makes our praise His throne
Behold the Lord our God will lead us home

© 2016 Hillsong Music Publishing.
All rights reserved. International copyright secured.
Used by permission.
Tel: +61 2 8853 5300
Email: publishing@hillsong.com
CCLI Song No. 7068430
Inspired by "How Great Thou Art!", courtesy of The Stuart Hine Trust

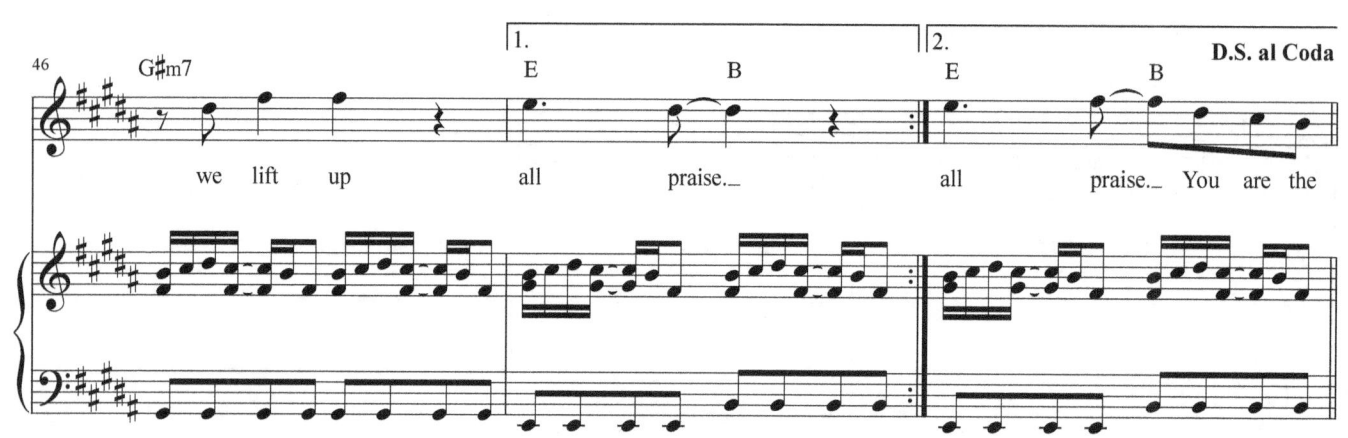

LOVE SO GREAT

**Words and Music by
JOSHUA GRIMMETT,
REUBEN MORGAN & JAMIE SNELL**

With energy ♩ = 92

Your love so great, Je-sus in all
Cre-a-tion calls, all to the Sav-

things, I've seen a glimpse of Your heart.
-iour. We are a-live for Your praise.

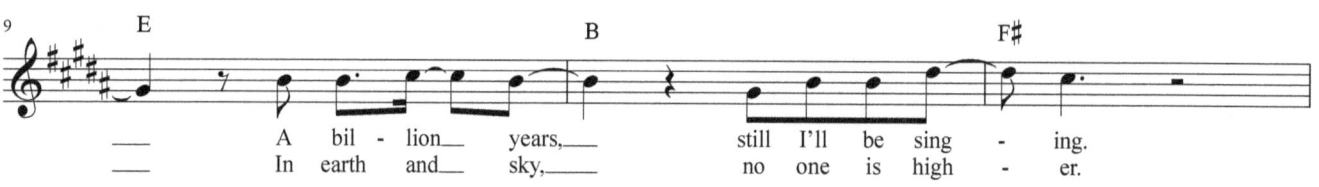

A bil-lion years, still I'll be sing-ing.
In earth and sky, no one is high-er.

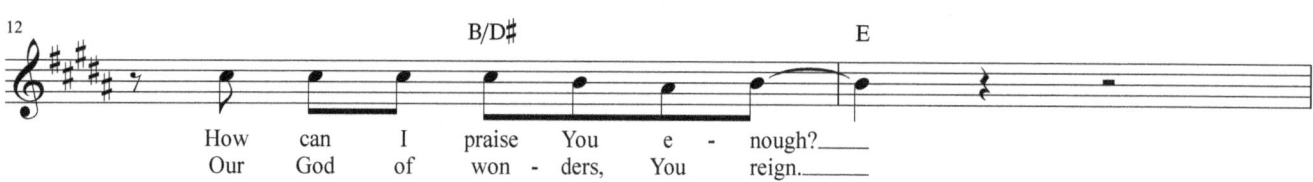

How can I praise You e-nough?
Our God of won-ders, You reign.

How can I praise You e-nough?
Our God of won-ders, You reign.
You are the

© 2016 Hillsong Music Publishing.
All rights reserved. International copyright secured. Used by permission.
Tel: +61 2 8853 5300 Email: publishing@hillsong.com CCLI Song No. 7068428

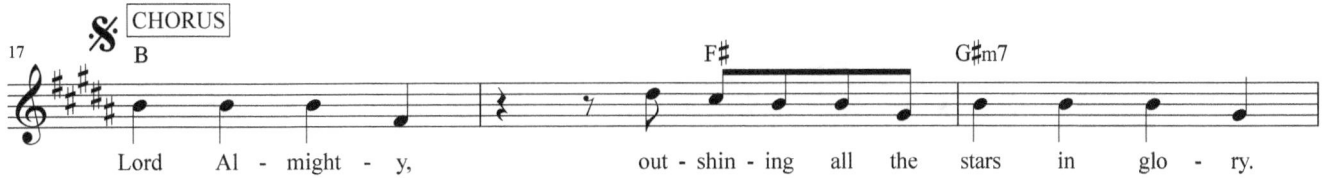
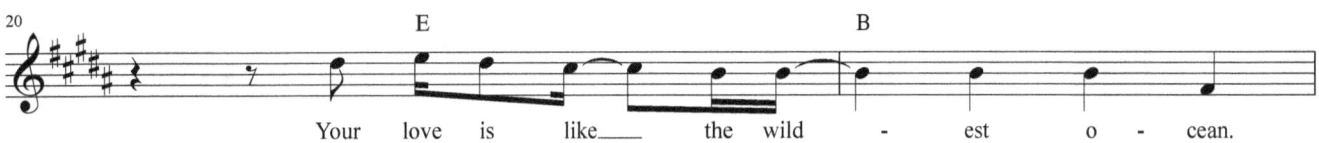

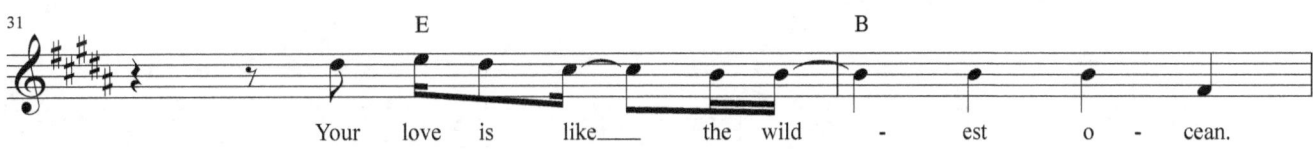

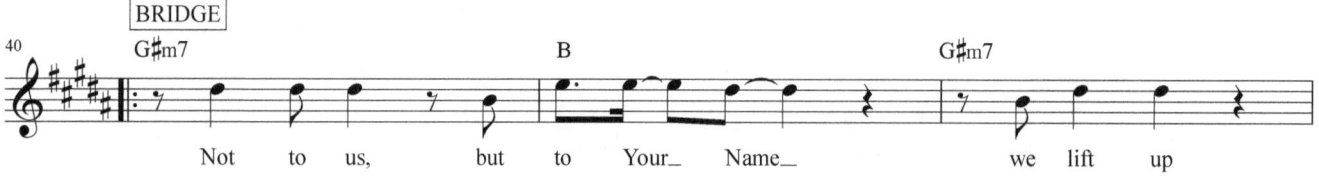
Not to us, but to Your Name we lift up

all praise. Not to us, but to Your Name

we lift up all praise. all praise. You are the

Not to us, but to Your Name

we lift up all praise. Not to us, but

LOVE SO GREAT

**Words and Music by Joshua Grimmett,
Reuben Morgan & Jamie Snell**

VERSE 1:
Your love so great
Jesus in all things
I've seen a glimpse of Your heart
A billion years
Still I'll be singing
How can I praise You enough

CHORUS:
You are the Lord Almighty
Out shining all the stars in glory
Your love is like the wildest ocean
Oh nothing else compares

VERSE 2:
Creation calls
All to the Saviour
We are alive for Your praise
In earth and sky no one is higher
Our God of wonders You reign

© 2016 Hillsong Music Publishing.
All rights reserved. International copyright secured.
Used by permission.
Tel: +61 2 8853 5300
Email: publishing@hillsong.com
CCLI Song No. 7068428

BRIDGE:
Not to us
But to Your Name
We lift up
All praise

© 2016 Hillsong Music Publishing.
All rights reserved. International copyright secured.
Used by permission.
Tel: +61 2 8853 5300
Email: publishing@hillsong.com
CCLI Song No. 7068428

LOOK TO THE SON

Words and Music by
MATT CROCKER, JOEL HOUSTON,
SCOTT LIGERTWOOD, REUBEN MORGAN
& MARTY SAMPSON

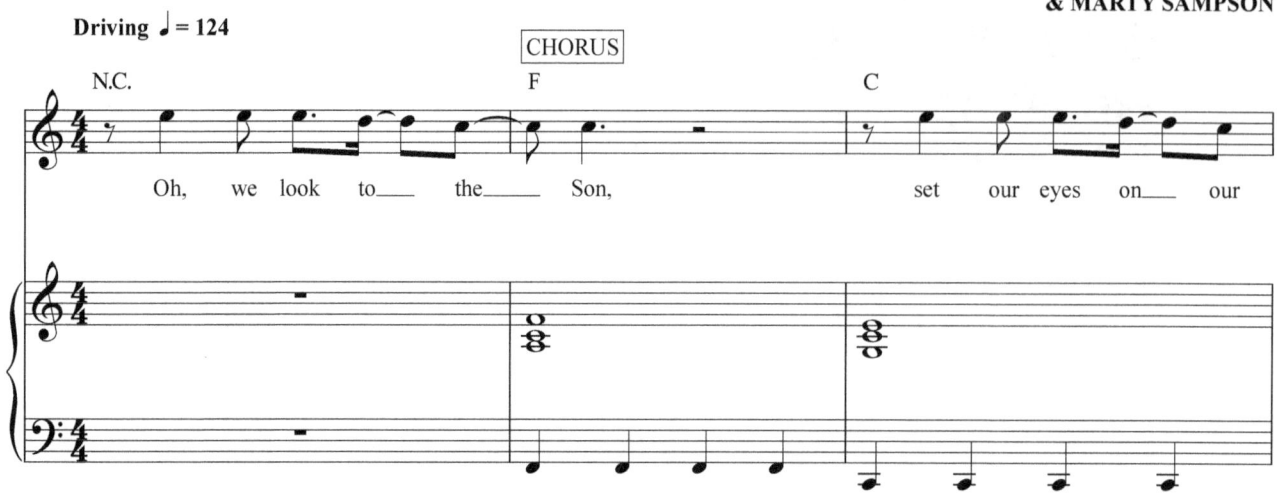

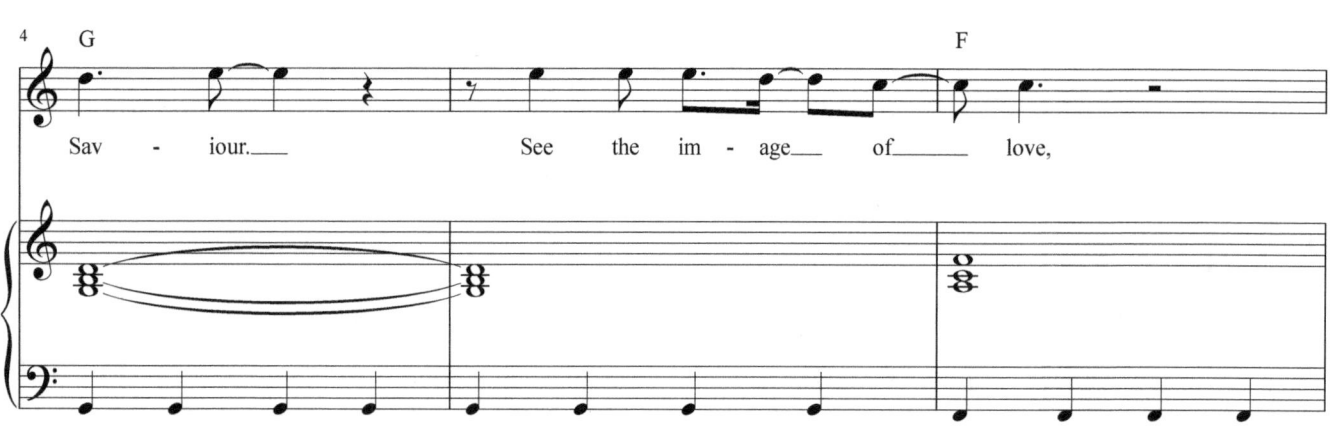

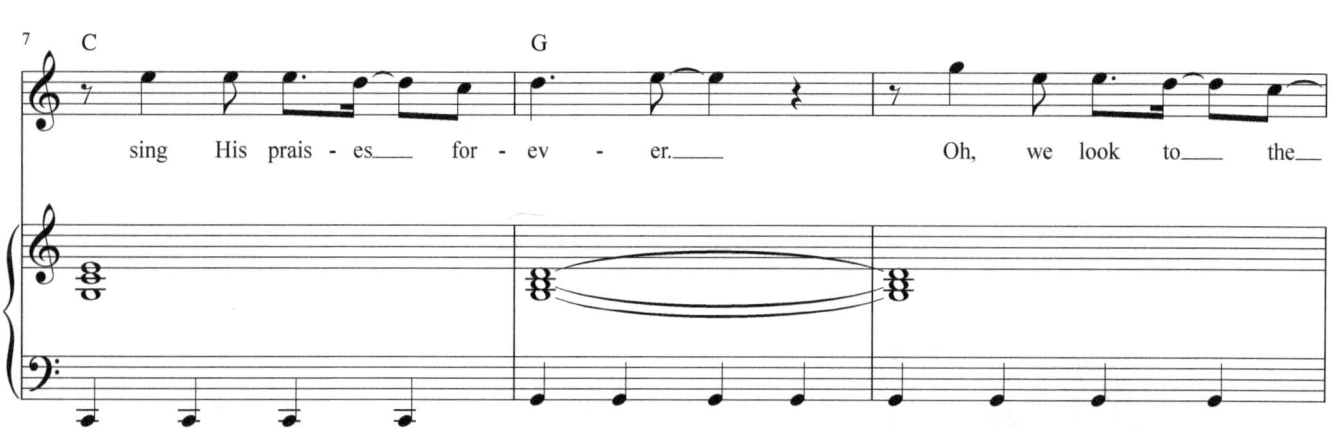

© 2016 Hillsong Music Publishing.
All rights reserved. International copyright secured. Used by permission.
Tel: +61 2 8853 5300   Email: publishing@hillsong.com   CCLI Song No. 7068422

LOOK TO THE SON

Words and Music by
MATT CROCKER, JOEL HOUSTON,
SCOTT LIGERTWOOD, REUBEN MORGAN
& MARTY SAMPSON

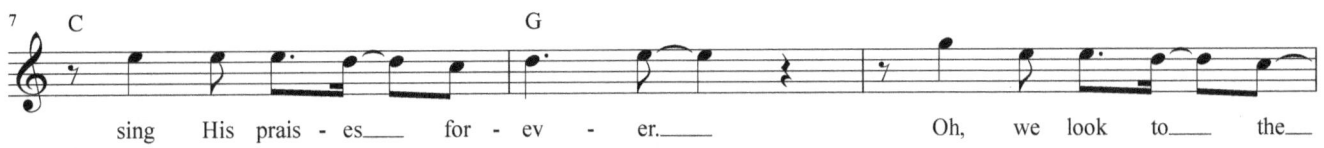

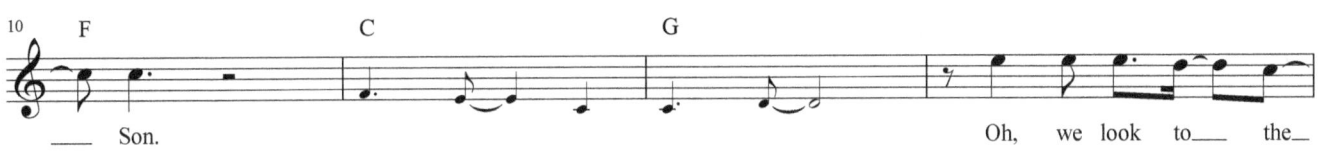

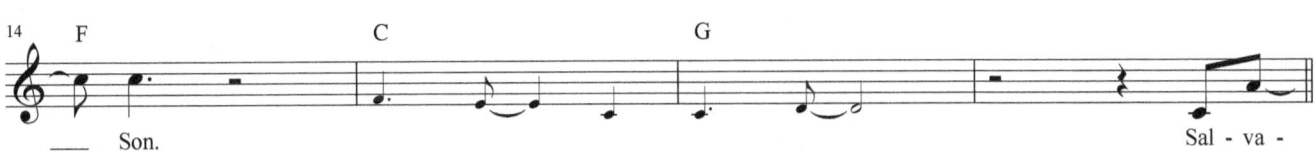

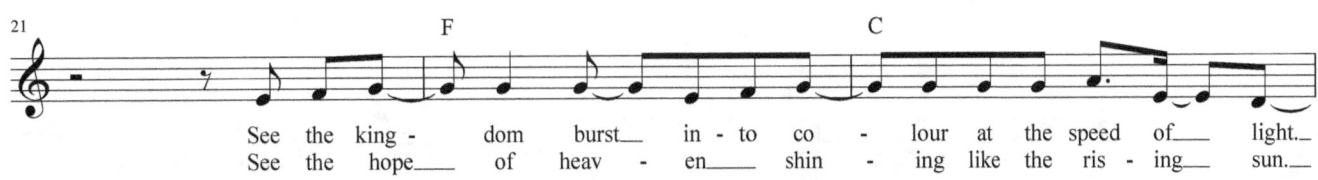

© 2016 Hillsong Music Publishing.
All rights reserved. International copyright secured. Used by permission.
Tel: +61 2 8853 5300 Email: publishing@hillsong.com CCLI Song No. 7068422

LOOK TO THE SON
Words and Music by Matthew Crocker, Joel Houston, Scott Ligertwood, Reuben Morgan & Marty Sampson

VERSE 1:
Salvation
Tearing through the dead of night
See the kingdom burst into colour
At the speed of light

Freedom
Shaking up the atmosphere
As the shadows fade into nothing
As the day appears

PRE-CHORUS:
Beyond the skies above
Love reaching out for us
The Everlasting One
Jesus our God

CHORUS:
We look to the Son
Set our eyes on our Saviour
See the image of love
Sing His praises forever

© 2016 Hillsong Music Publishing.
All rights reserved. International copyright secured.
Used by permission.
Tel: +61 2 8853 5300
Email: publishing@hillsong.com
CCLI Song No. 7068422

VERSE 2:

Creation
Waking up to kingdom come
See the hope of heaven
Shining like the rising sun

Now forever
Lifted up from death to life
There's no fear in love
And no darkness in His endless light

© 2016 Hillsong Music Publishing.
All rights reserved. International copyright secured.
Used by permission.
Tel: +61 2 8853 5300
Email: publishing@hillsong.com
CCLI Song No. 7068422

CROWNS

Words and Music by
MICHAEL FATKIN, SCOTT GROOM
& BENJAMIN HASTINGS

Worship ballad ♩ = 70

There is a hill I cherish where stood a precious tree.
How is it I should profit while He is crucified.

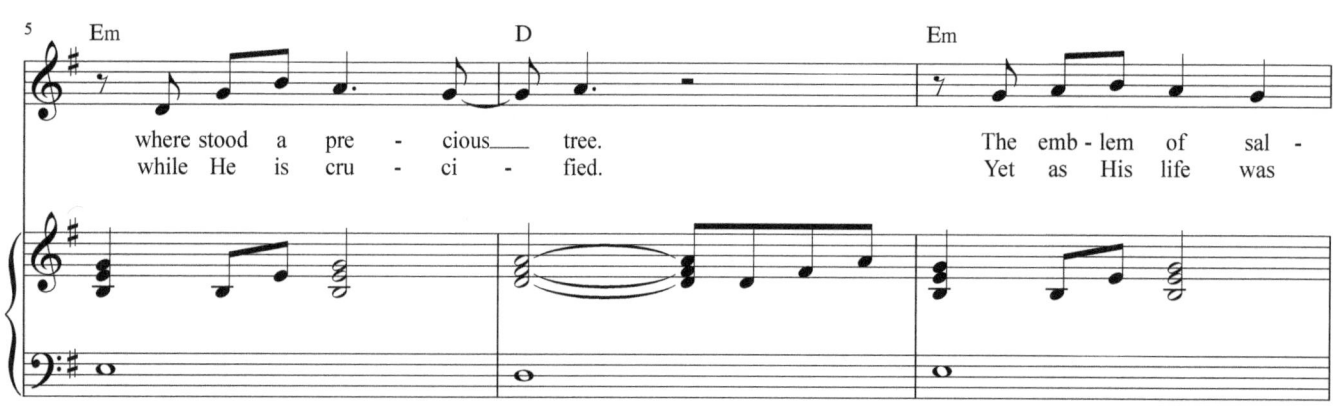

The emblem of salvation, the gift of Calvary.
Yet as His life was taken, so I was granted

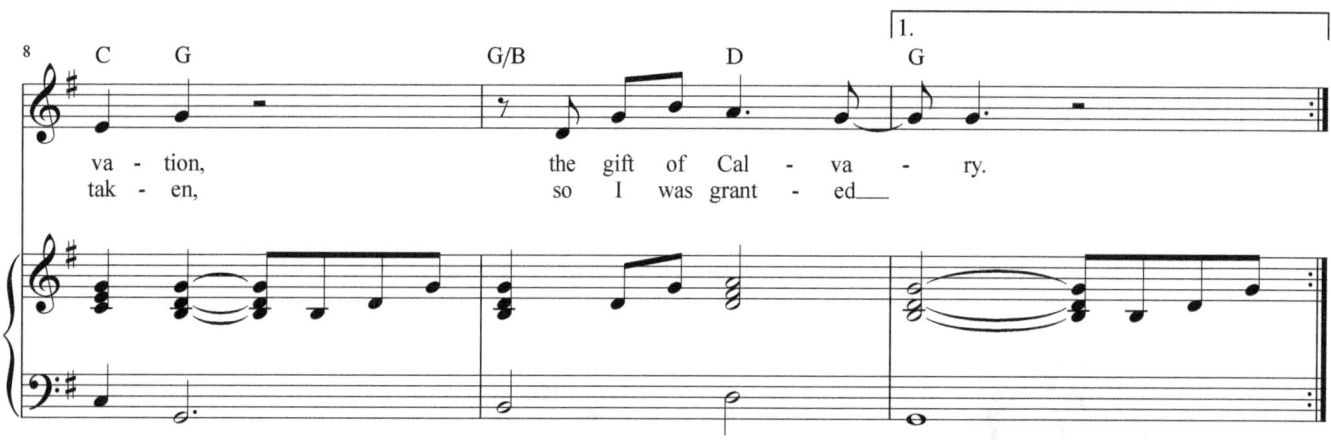

© 2016 Hillsong Music Publishing.
All rights reserved. International copyright secured. Used by permission.
Tel: +61 2 8853 5300   Email: publishing@hillsong.com   CCLI Song No. 7068421

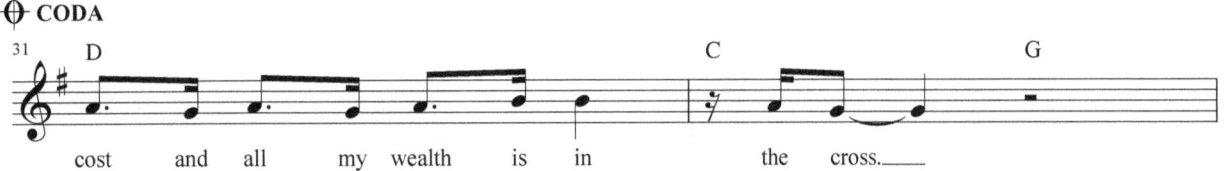
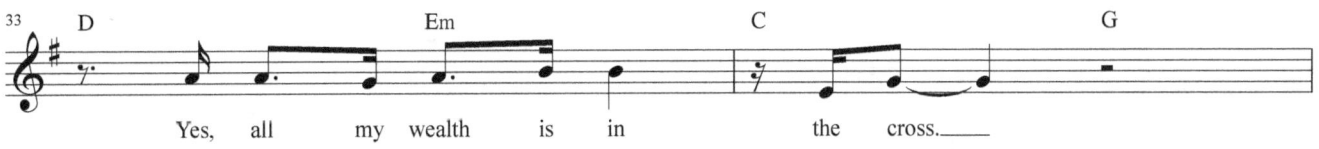
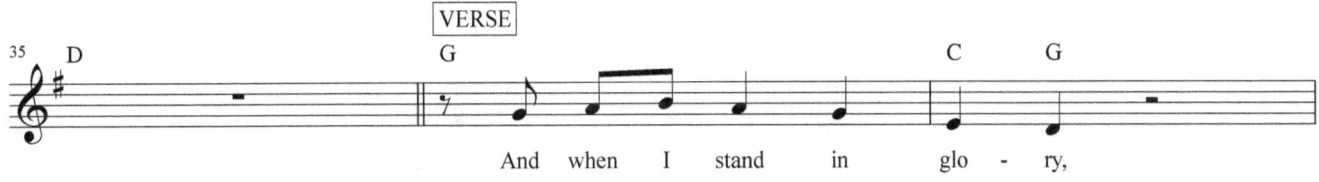
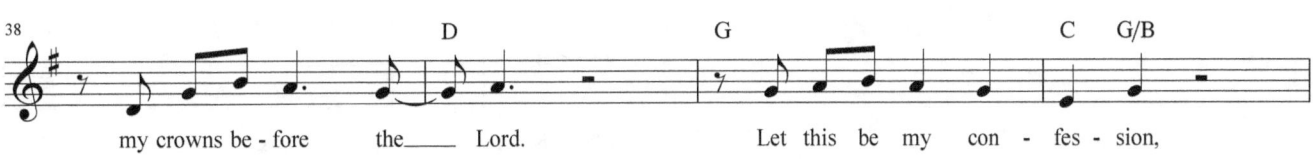
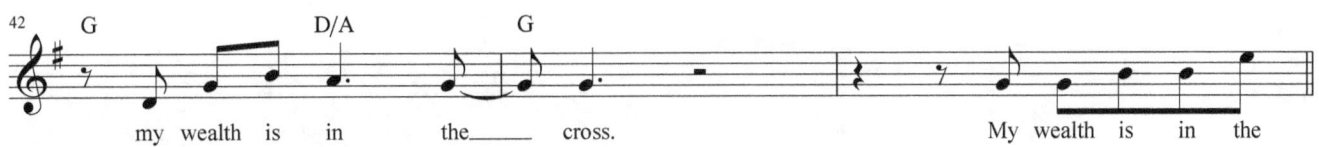

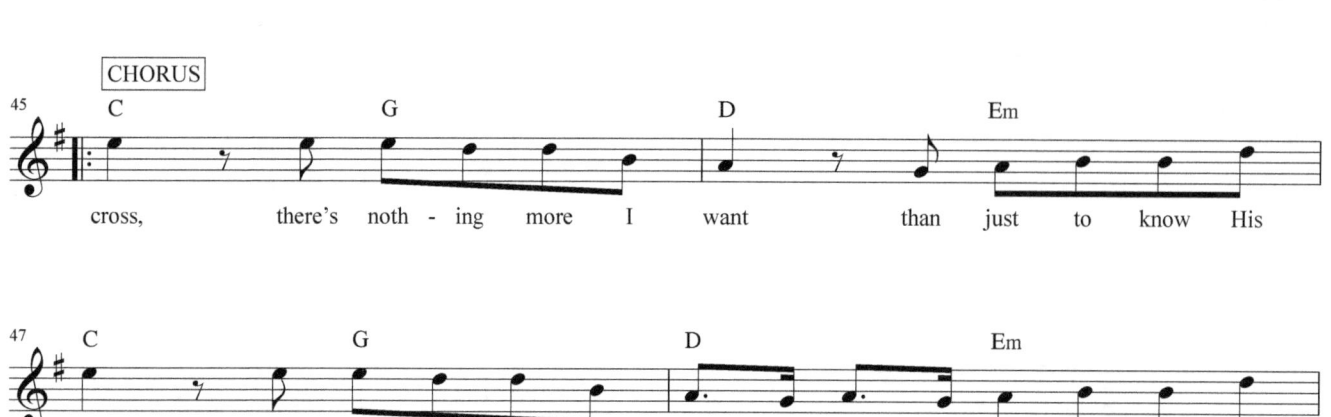

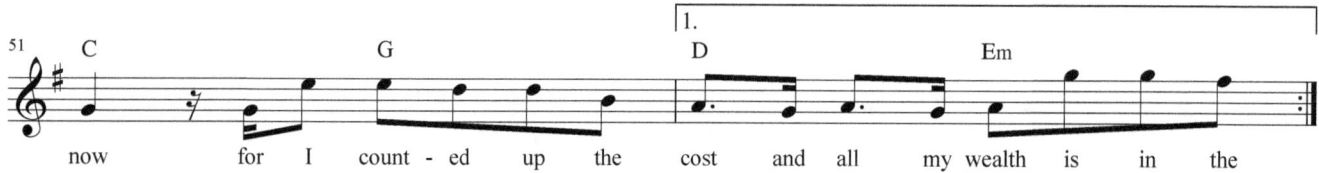
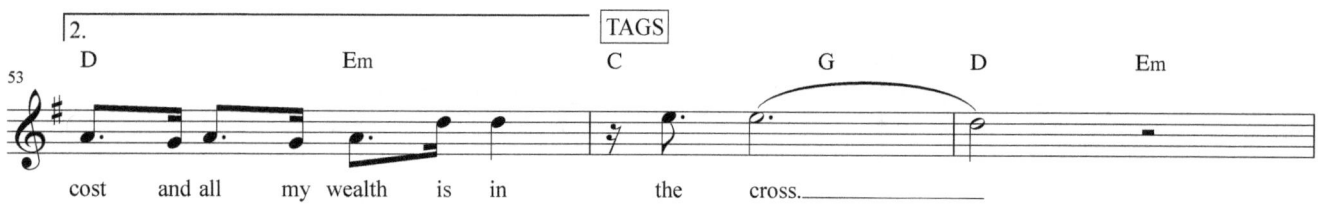

CROWNS

**Words and Music by
Michael Fatkin, Scott Groom & Benjamin Hastings**

VERSE 1:
There is a hill I cherish
Where stood a precious tree
The emblem of salvation
The gift of Calvary

VERSE 2:
How is it I should profit
While He is crucified
Yet as His life was taken
So I was granted mine

CHORUS:
My wealth is in the cross
There's nothing more I want
Than just to know His love
My heart is set on Christ
And I will count all else as loss
The greatest of my crowns
Mean nothing to me now
For I counted up the cost
And all my wealth is in the cross

© 2016 Hillsong Music Publishing.
All rights reserved. International copyright secured.
Used by permission.
Tel: +61 2 8853 5300
Email: publishing@hillsong.com
CCLI Song No. 7068421

VERSE 3:
I will not boast in riches
I have no pride in gold
But I will boast in Jesus
And in His Name alone

VERSE 4:
And when I stand in glory
My crowns before the Lord
Let this be my confession
My wealth is in the cross

© 2016 Hillsong Music Publishing.
All rights reserved. International copyright secured.
Used by permission.
Tel: +61 2 8853 5300
Email: publishing@hillsong.com
CCLI Song No. 7068421

WHAT A BEAUTIFUL NAME

**Words and Music by
BEN FIELDING &
BROOKE LIGERTWOOD**

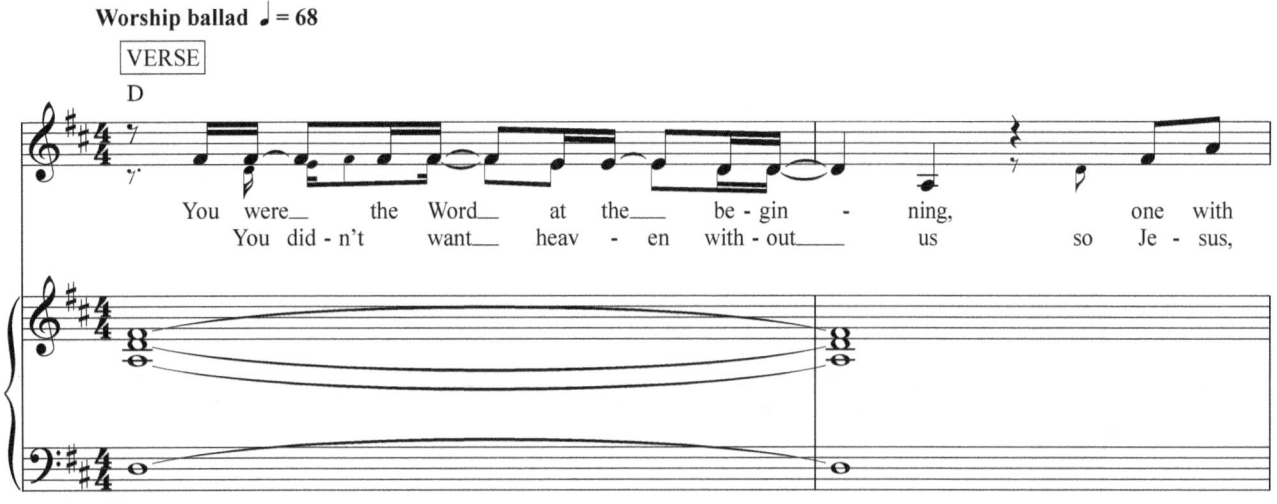

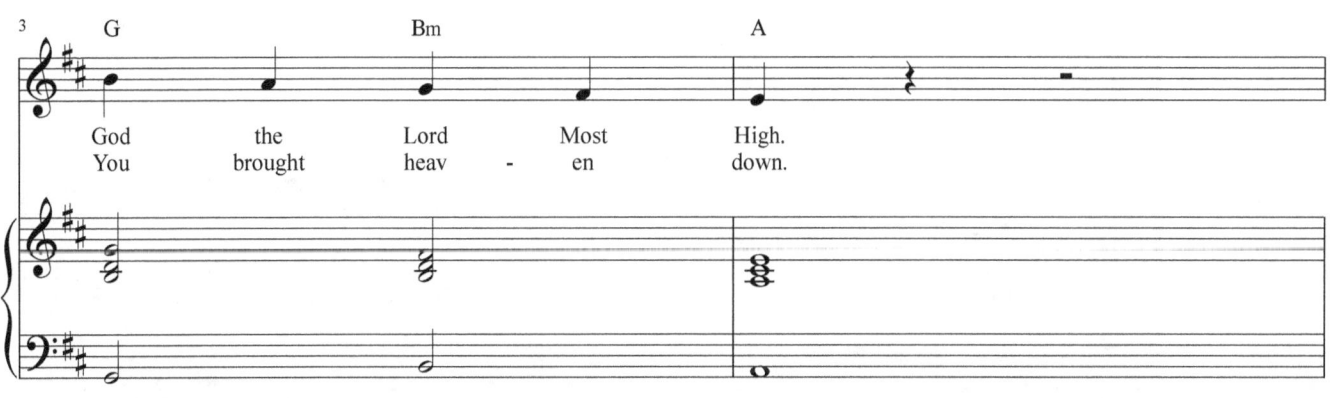

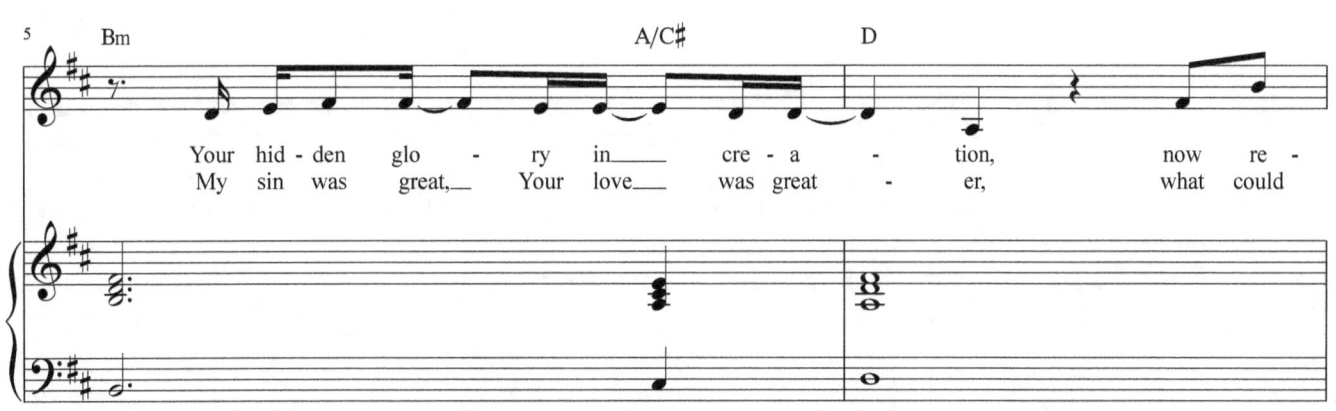

© 2016 Hillsong Music Publishing.
All rights reserved. International copyright secured. Used by permission.
Tel: +61 2 8853 5300 Email: publishing@hillsong.com CCLI Song No. 7068424

WHAT A BEAUTIFUL NAME

**Words and Music by
BEN FIELDING &
BROOKE LIGERTWOOD**

WHAT A BEAUTIFUL NAME

**Words and Music by
Ben Fielding & Brooke Ligertwood**

VERSE 1:
You were the Word at the beginning
One with God the Lord Most High
Your hidden glory in creation
Now revealed in You our Christ

CHORUS 1:
What a beautiful Name it is
What a beautiful Name it is
The Name of Jesus Christ my King
What a beautiful Name it is
Nothing compares to this
What a beautiful Name it is
The Name of Jesus

VERSE 2:
You didn't want heaven without us
So Jesus You brought heaven down
My sin was great Your love was greater
What could separate us now

© 2016 Hillsong Music Publishing.
All rights reserved. International copyright secured.
Used by permission.
Tel: +61 2 8853 5300
Email: publishing@hillsong.com
CCLI Song No. 7068424

CHORUS 2:
**What a wonderful Name it is
What a wonderful Name it is
The Name of Jesus Christ my King
What a wonderful Name it is
Nothing compares to this
What a wonderful Name it is
The Name of Jesus
What a wonderful Name it is
The Name of Jesus**

BRIDGE:
**Death could not hold You
The veil tore before You
You silence the boast of sin and grave
The heavens are roaring
The praise of Your glory
For You are raised to life again**

**You have no rival
You have no equal
Now and forever God You reign
Yours is the kingdom
Yours is the glory
Yours is the Name above all names**

© 2016 Hillsong Music Publishing.
All rights reserved. International copyright secured.
Used by permission.
Tel: +61 2 8853 5300
Email: publishing@hillsong.com
CCLI Song No. 7068424

CHORUS 3:
What a powerful Name it is
What a powerful Name it is
The Name of Jesus Christ my King
What a powerful Name it is
Nothing can stand against
What a powerful Name it is
The Name of Jesus

TAGS:
What a powerful Name it is
The Name of Jesus
What a powerful Name it is
The Name of Jesus

© 2016 Hillsong Music Publishing.
All rights reserved. International copyright secured.
Used by permission.
Tel: +61 2 8853 5300
Email: publishing@hillsong.com
CCLI Song No. 7068424

YOUR WORD

Words and Music by
CHRIS DAVENPORT

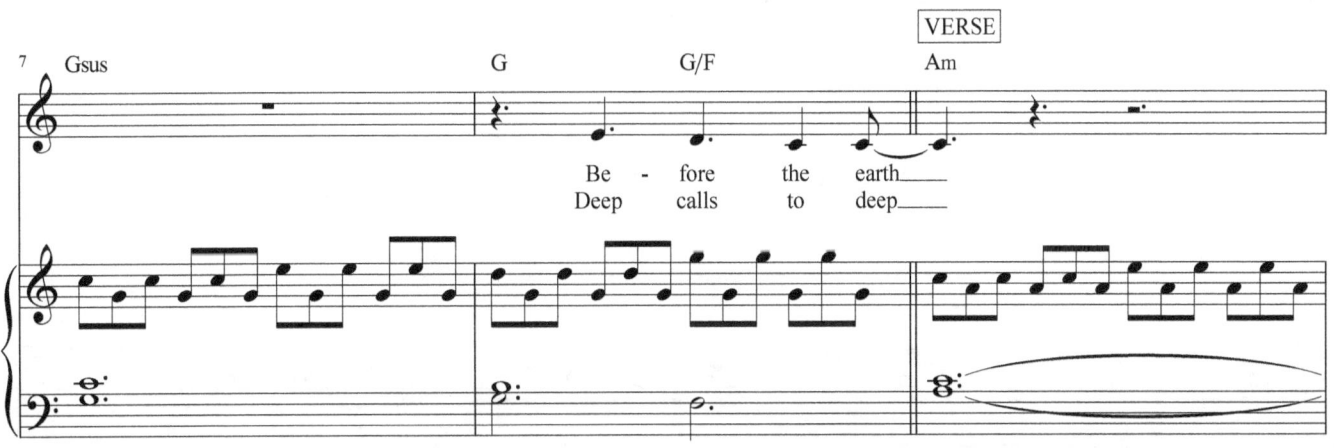

© 2016 Hillsong Music Publishing.
All rights reserved. International copyright secured. Used by permission.
Tel: +61 2 8853 5300 Email: publishing@hillsong.com CCLI Song No. 7068426

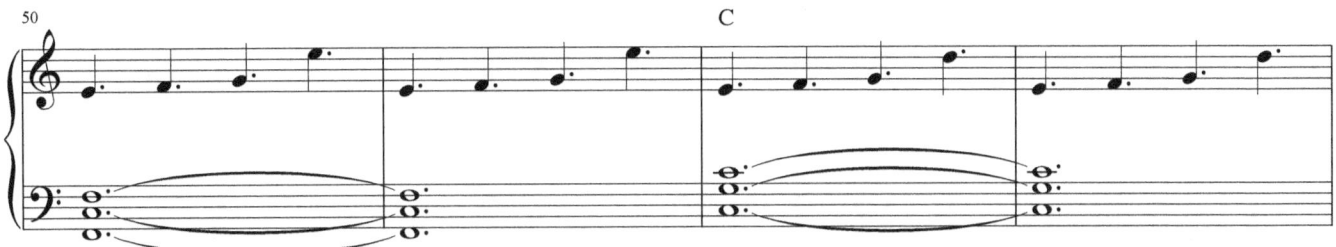
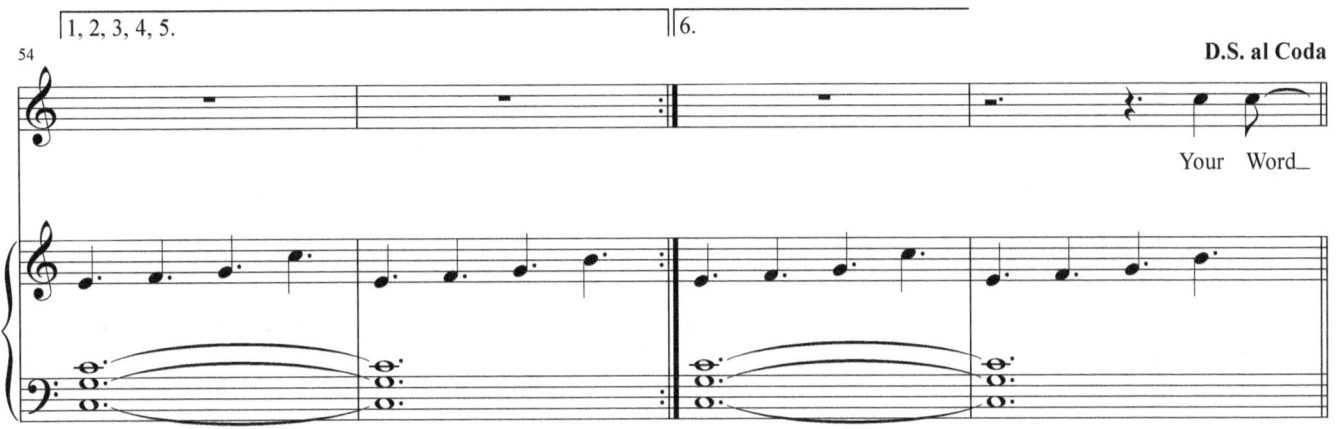
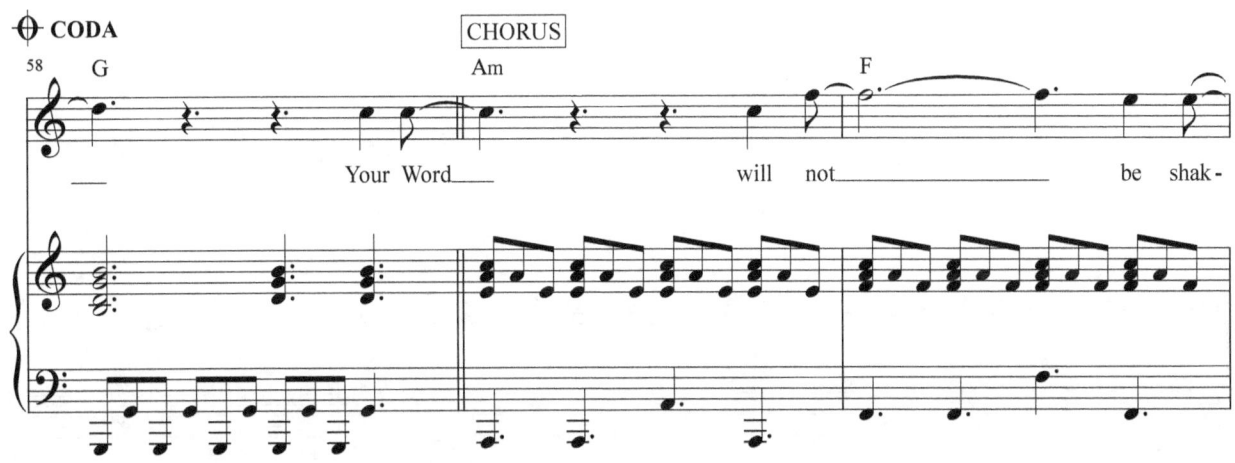

YOUR WORD

Words and Music by
CHRIS DAVENPORT

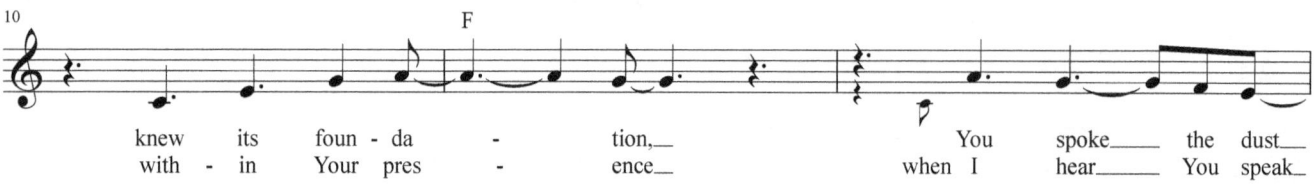
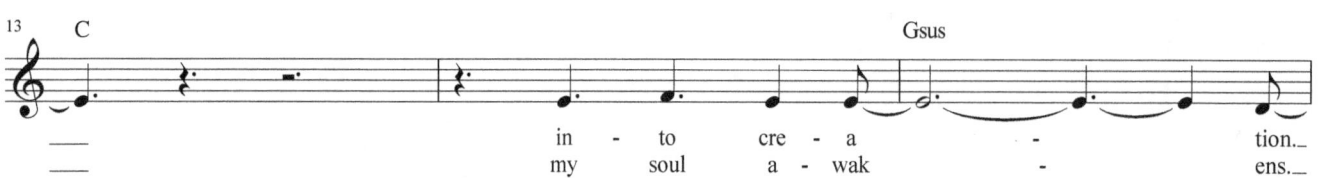

© 2016 Hillsong Music Publishing.
All rights reserved. International copyright secured. Used by permission.
Tel: +61 2 8853 5300 Email: publishing@hillsong.com CCLI Song No. 7068426

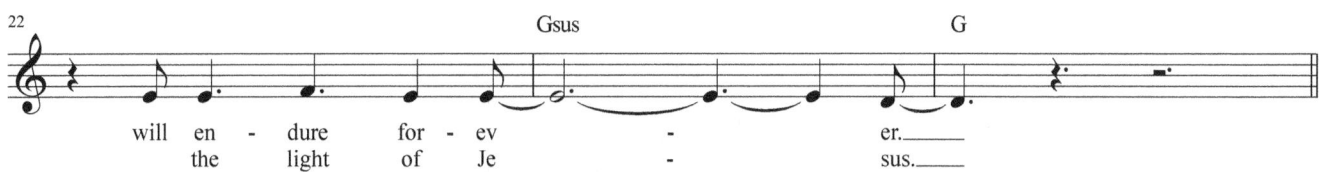

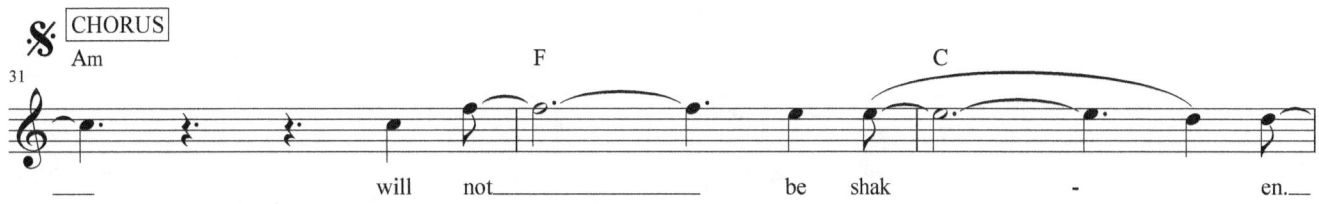

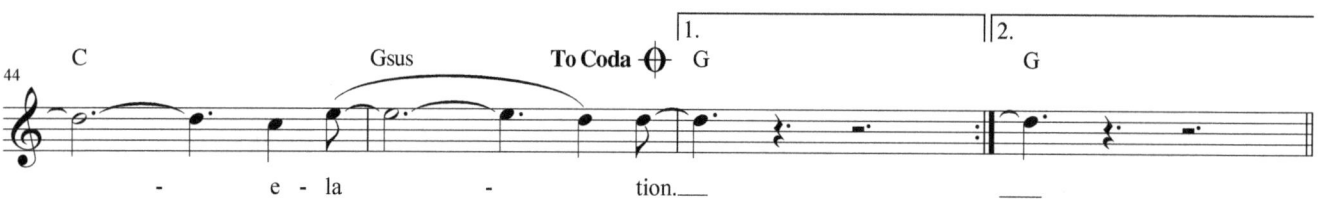

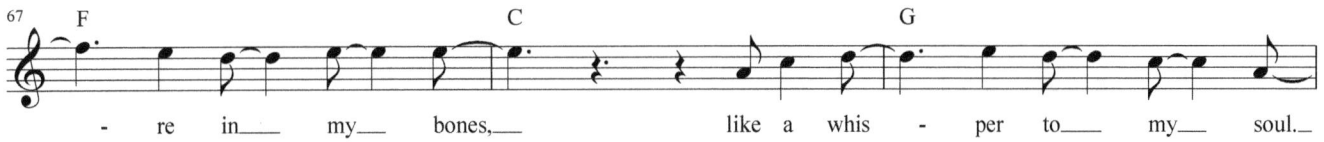

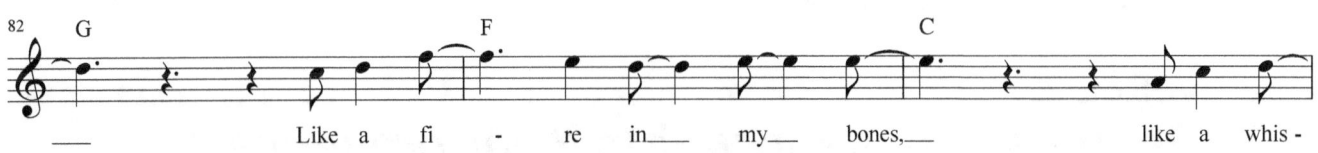

YOUR WORD

Words and Music by Chris Davenport

VERSE 1:
Before the earth knew its foundation
You spoke the dust into creation
Until the end when all has withered
Then still Your Word will endure forever

PRE-CHORUS:
The lamp unto my feet
The light unto my path

CHORUS:
Your Word will not be shaken
Your Word will never fail me
Like a fire in my bones
Like a whisper to my soul
Your Word is revelation

VERSE 2:
Deep calls to deep within Your presence
When I hear You speak my soul awakens
Your Spirit leads my heart to worship
As Your Word reveals the light of Jesus

© 2016 Hillsong Music Publishing.
All rights reserved. International copyright secured.
Used by permission.
Tel: +61 2 8853 5300
Email: publishing@hillsong.com
CCLI Song No. 7068426

LET THERE BE LIGHT

**Words and Music by
MICHAEL GUY CHISLETT, MATT CROCKER,
JOEL HOUSTON, BROOKE LIGERTWOOD
& SCOTT LIGERTWOOD**

LET THERE BE LIGHT

**Words and Music by
MICHAEL GUY CHISLETT, MATT CROCKER,
JOEL HOUSTON, BROOKE LIGERTWOOD
& SCOTT LIGERTWOOD**

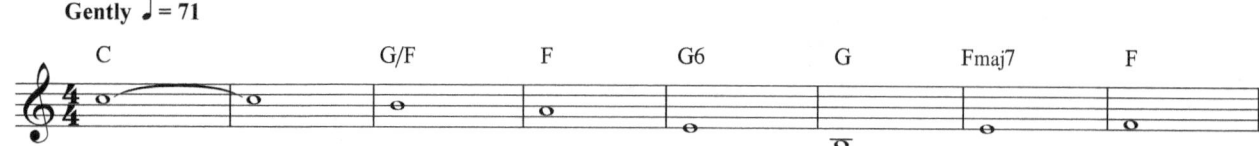

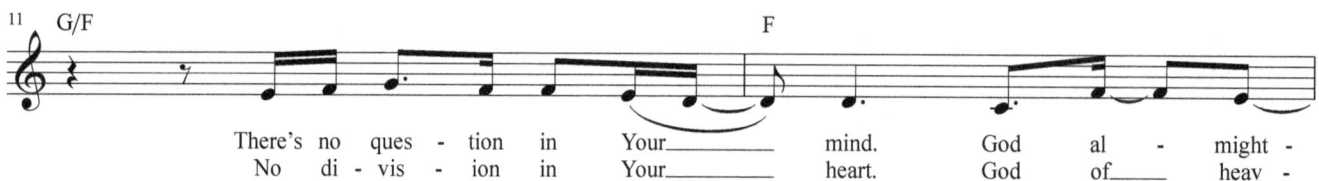

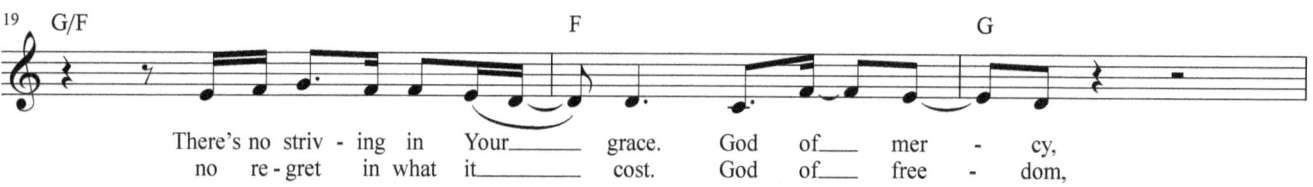

© 2016 Hillsong Music Publishing.
All rights reserved. International copyright secured. Used by permission.
Tel: +61 2 8853 5300 Email: publishing@hillsong.com CCLI Song No. 7069096

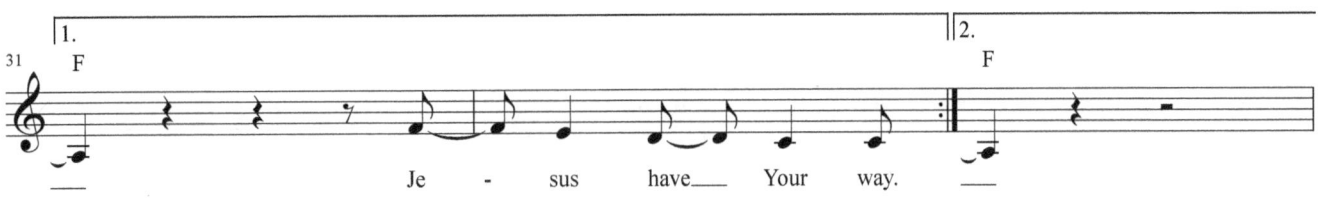

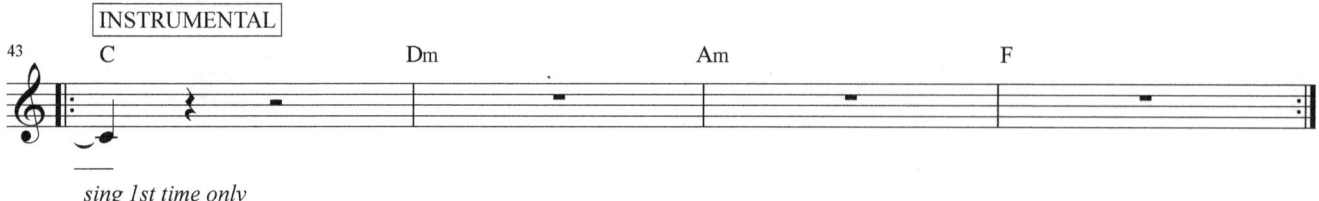

sing 1st time only

Good news em-brac-ing the poor, com-fort for all those who mourn.

For the bro-ken heart-ed we sing loud-er. Re-lease from pri-son and shame,

op-pres-sion turn-ing to praise. For ev-'ry cap-tive, sing loud-er.

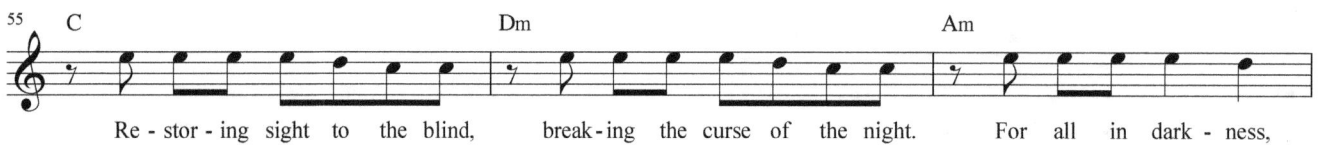

Re-stor-ing sight to the blind, break-ing the curse of the night. For all in dark-ness,

sing loud-er. Pro-claim-ing free-dom for all, this is the day of the Lord.

Beau-ty for ash-es. Let there be light.

LET THERE BE LIGHT

Words and Music by Michael Guy Chislett, Matthew Crocker, Joel Houston, Brooke Ligertwood & Scott Ligertwood

VERSE 1:
There's no darkness in Your eyes
There's no question in Your mind
God almighty
God of mercy

There's no hiding from Your face
There's no striving in Your grace
God of mercy
God almighty

CHORUS 1:
Let there be light
Open the eyes of the blind
Purify our hearts in Your fire
Breathe in us we pray
Jesus have Your way

© 2016 Hillsong Music Publishing.
All rights reserved. International copyright secured.
Used by permission.
Tel: +61 2 8853 5300
Email: publishing@hillsong.com
CCLI Song No. 7069096

VERSE 2:
There's no borders in Your love
No division in Your heart
God of heaven
God of freedom

There's no taking back the cross
No regret in what it cost
God of freedom
God of heaven

CHORUS 2:
Let there be light
Open the eyes of the blind
Purify our hearts in Your fire
Breathe in us we pray

Let there be light
Open our eyes to Your heart
Desperate just to know who You are
Shine in us we pray
Jesus have Your way

© 2016 Hillsong Music Publishing.
All rights reserved. International copyright secured.
Used by permission.
Tel: +61 2 8853 5300
Email: publishing@hillsong.com
CCLI Song No. 7069096

BRIDGE:
Good news embracing the poor
Comfort for all those who mourn
For the broken hearted
We sing louder

Release from prison and shame
Oppression turning to praise
For every captive
Sing louder

Restoring sight to the blind
Breaking the curse of the night
For all in darkness
Sing louder

Proclaiming freedom for all
This is the day of the Lord
Beauty for ashes

VERSE 3:
Let the light that shines above
Become the light that shines in us
There's no darkness in Your way
So have Your way
Lord have Your way

© 2016 Hillsong Music Publishing.
All rights reserved. International copyright secured.
Used by permission.
Tel: +61 2 8853 5300
Email: publishing@hillsong.com
CCLI Song No. 7069096

IN CONTROL

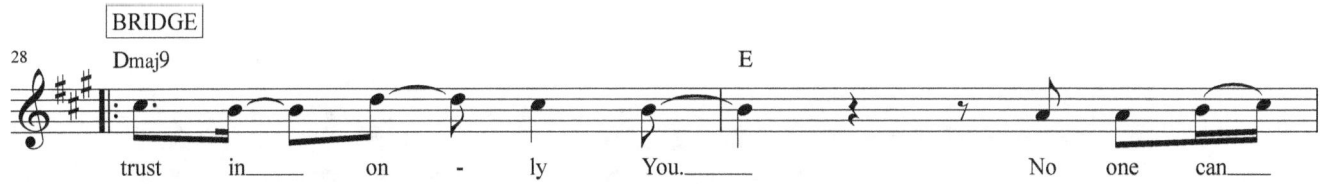

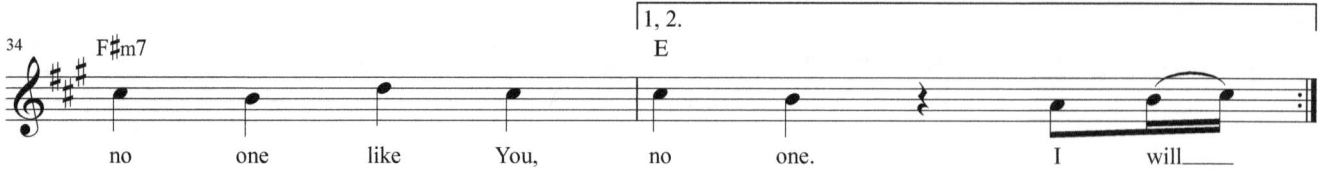
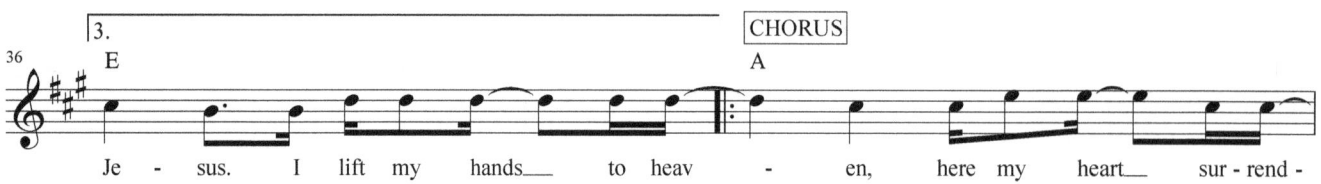
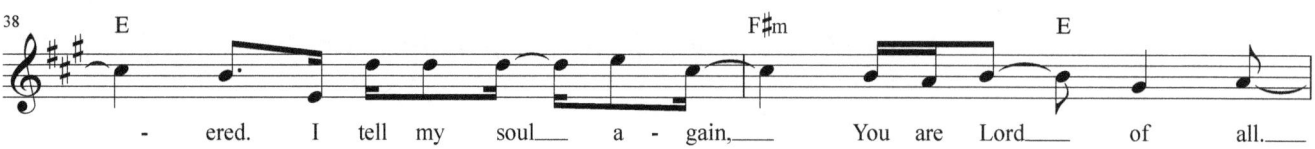
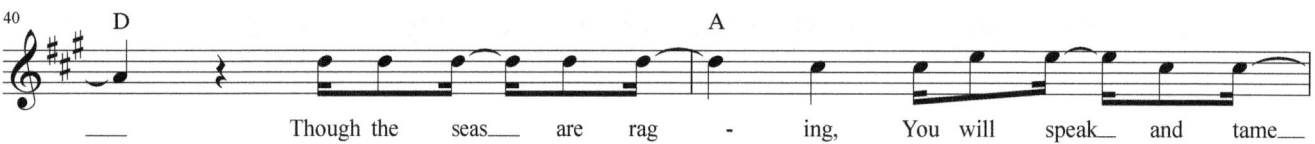

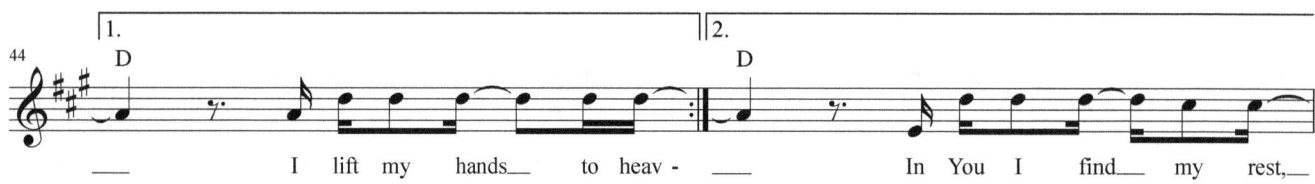

IN CONTROL

**Words and Music by
Ben Fielding & Aodhan King**

VERSE 1:
From heaven You can hear
I know You're drawing near
As I worship
Held within Your love
The wind and waves will come
But I will stay here

CHORUS:
I lift my hands to heaven
Here my heart surrendered
I tell my soul again
You are Lord of all
Though the seas are raging
You will speak and tame them
In You I find my rest
You are in control

© 2016 Hillsong Music Publishing.
All rights reserved. International copyright secured.
Used by permission.
Tel: +61 2 8853 5300
Email: publishing@hillsong.com
CCLI Song No. 7068425

VERSE 2:
Through valleys I will trust
Your Spirit is enough to keep me walking
You guide my every step
Speak life to me again
Lord I need You

BRIDGE:
I will trust in only You
No one can add to Your perfection
You're the beginning and the end
More than I can comprehend
There is no one like You

No one
No one
No one Jesus

© 2016 Hillsong Music Publishing.
All rights reserved. International copyright secured.
Used by permission.
Tel: +61 2 8853 5300
Email: publishing@hillsong.com
CCLI Song No. 7068425

GRACE TO GRACE

31
2.
C
F
to grace.
BRIDGE
34
B♭
Dm
When I see that cross, I see free - dom.
When I see that grave, I'll see Je - sus.
36
F
C
And from death to life, I will sing Your praise
in the won - der of Your grace.
38
B♭
Dm
When I see that cross, I see free - dom.
When I see that grave, I'll see Je - sus.

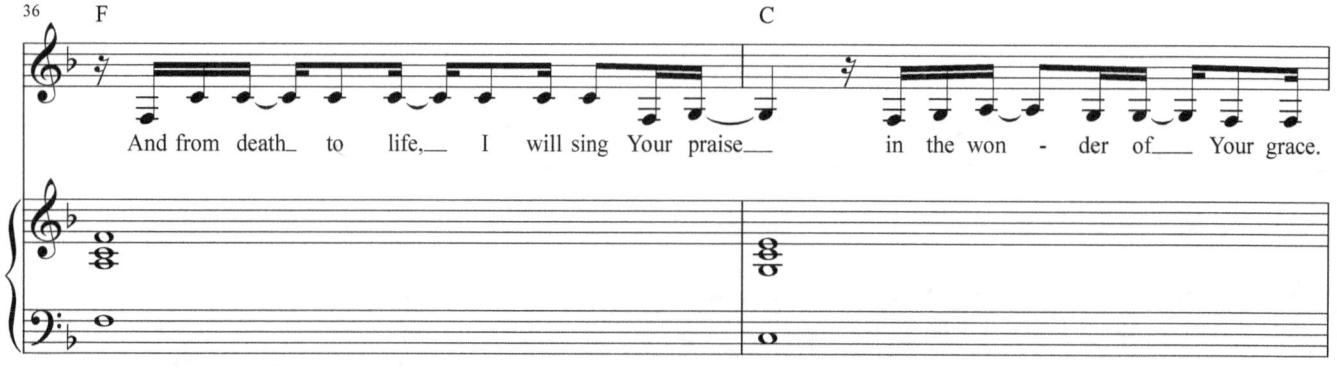

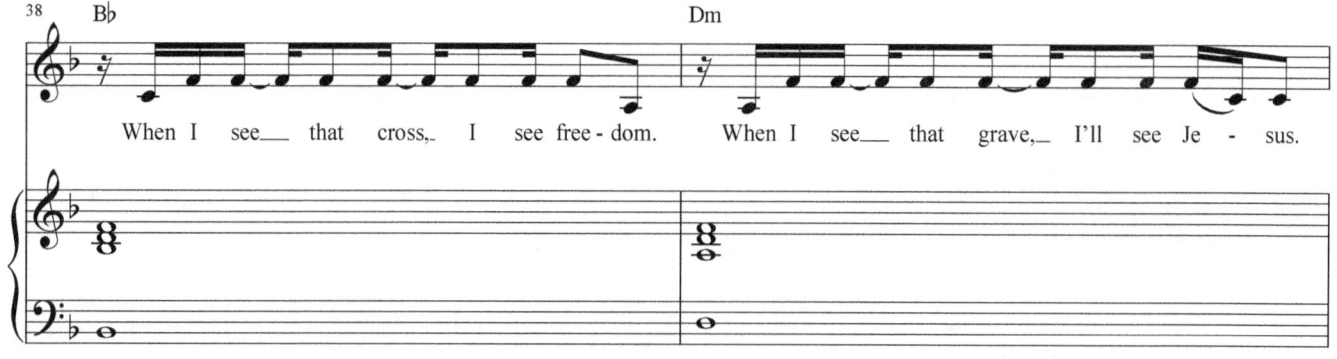

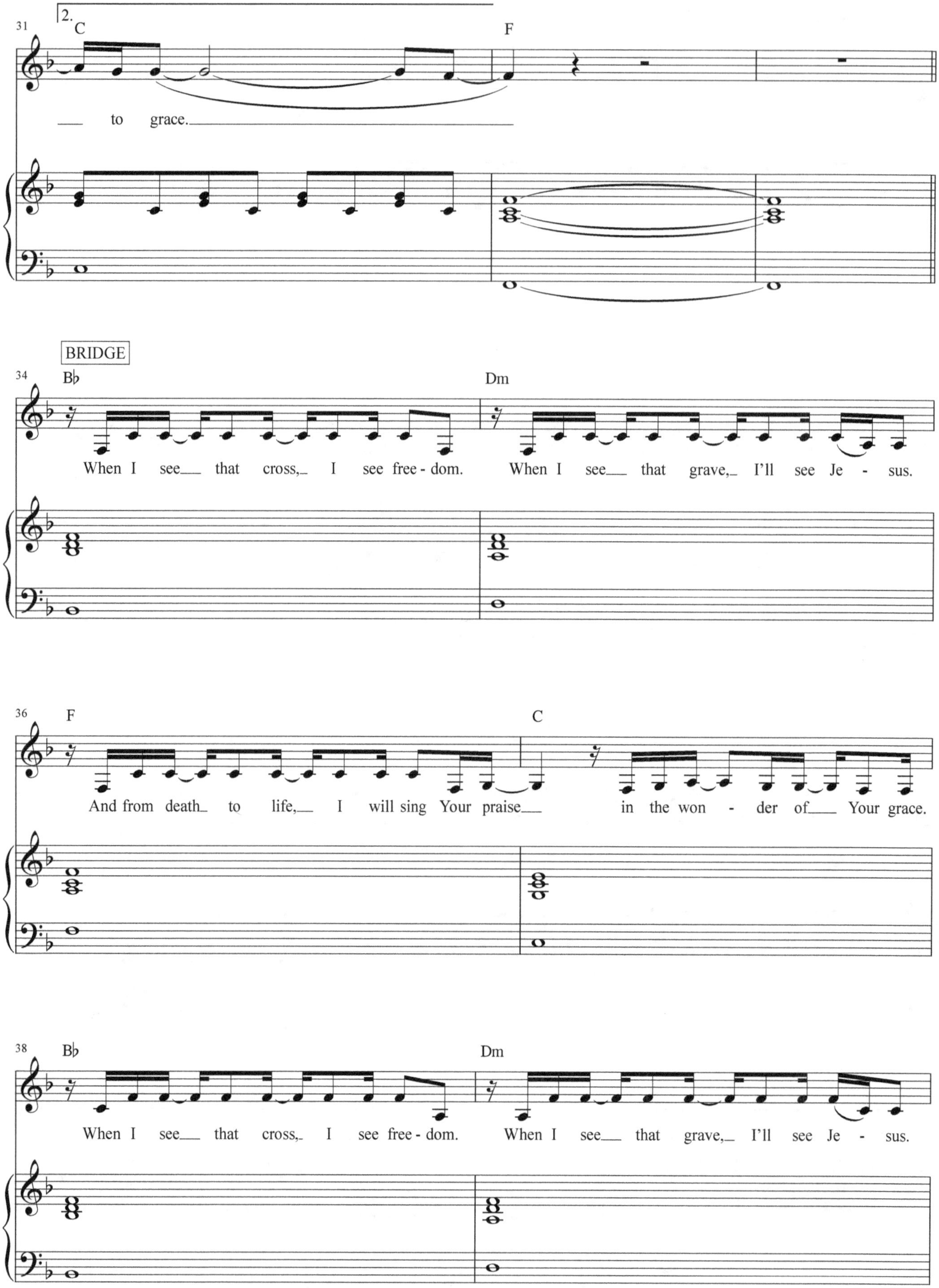

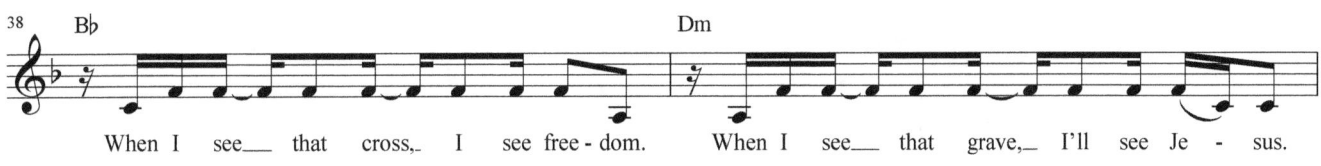
When I see that cross, I see free-dom. When I see that grave, I'll see Je-sus.

And from death to life, I will sing Your praise in the won-der of Your grace.

BRIDGE

When I see that cross, I see free-dom. When I see that grave, I'll see Je-sus.

And from death to life, I will sing Your praise in the won-der of Your grace.

TAG

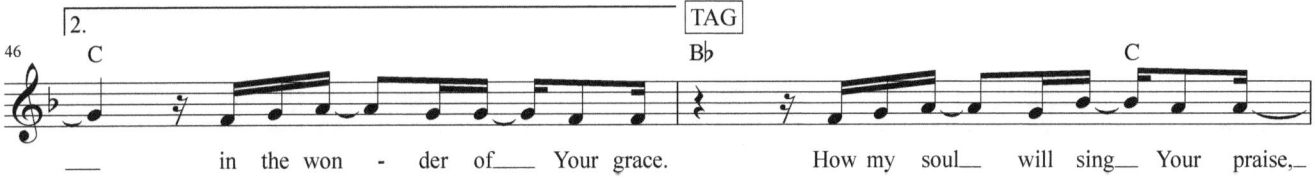
in the won-der of Your grace. How my soul will sing Your praise,

in the won-der of Your grace. How my soul will sing Your praise.

CHORUS

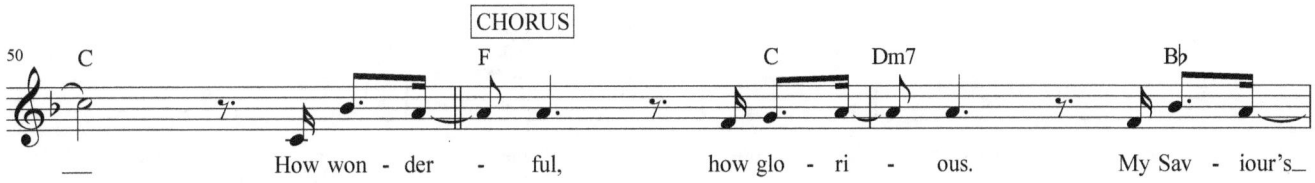
How won-der-ful, how glo-ri-ous. My Sav-iour's

scars, vic-to-ri-ous. My chains are gone, my debt is

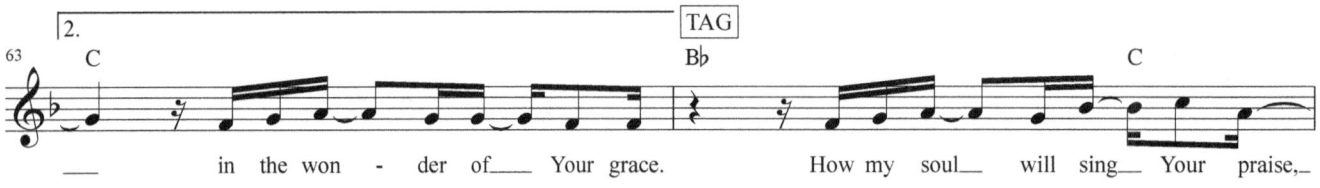
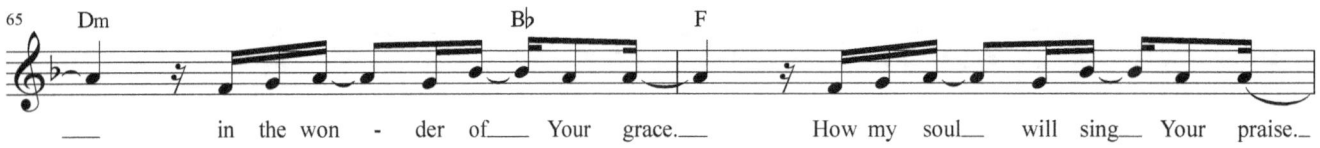
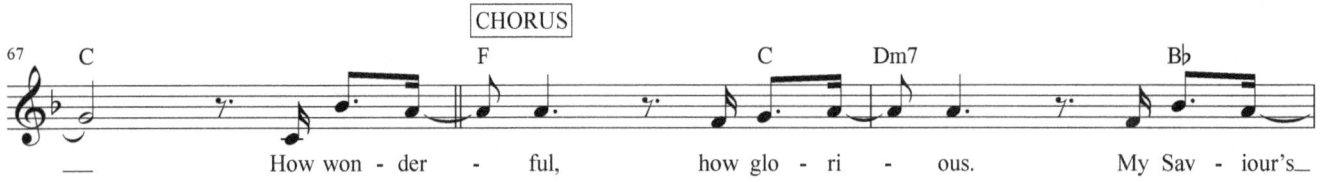
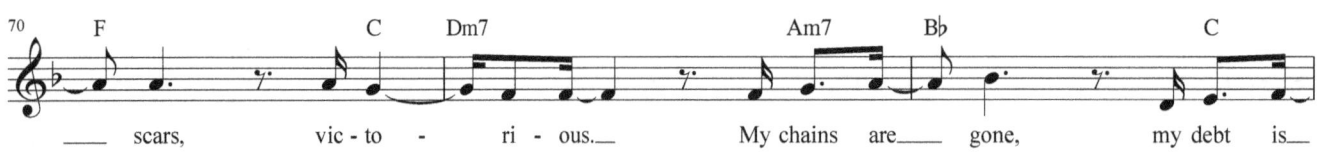

GRACE TO GRACE

**Words and Music by
Chris Davenport & Joel Houston**

VERSE 1:
If love endured that ancient cross
How precious is my Saviour's blood
The beauty of heaven wrapped in my shame
The image of love upon death's frame

PRE-CHORUS 1:
If having my heart was worth the pain
What joy could You see beyond the grave
If love found my soul worth dying for

CHORUS:
How wonderful
How glorious
My Saviour's scars
Victorious
My chains are gone
My debt is paid
From death to life
And grace to grace

© 2016 Hillsong Music Publishing.
All rights reserved. International copyright secured.
Used by permission.
Tel: +61 2 8853 5300
Email: publishing@hillsong.com
CCLI Song No. 7057218

VERSE 2:

If heaven now owns that vacant tomb
How great is the hope that lives in You
The passion that tore through hell like a rose
The promise that rolled back death and its stone

PRE-CHORUS 2:

If freedom is worth the life You raised
Oh where is my sin where is my shame
If love paid it all to have my heart

BRIDGE:

When I see that cross I see freedom
When I see that grave I'll see Jesus
And from death to life I will sing Your praise
In the wonder of Your grace

TAGS:

How my soul will sing Your praise
In the wonder of Your grace
How my soul will sing Your praise

© 2016 Hillsong Music Publishing.
All rights reserved. International copyright secured.
Used by permission.
Tel: +61 2 8853 5300
Email: publishing@hillsong.com
CCLI Song No. 7057218

ELOHIM

**Words and Music by
MARTY SAMPSON**

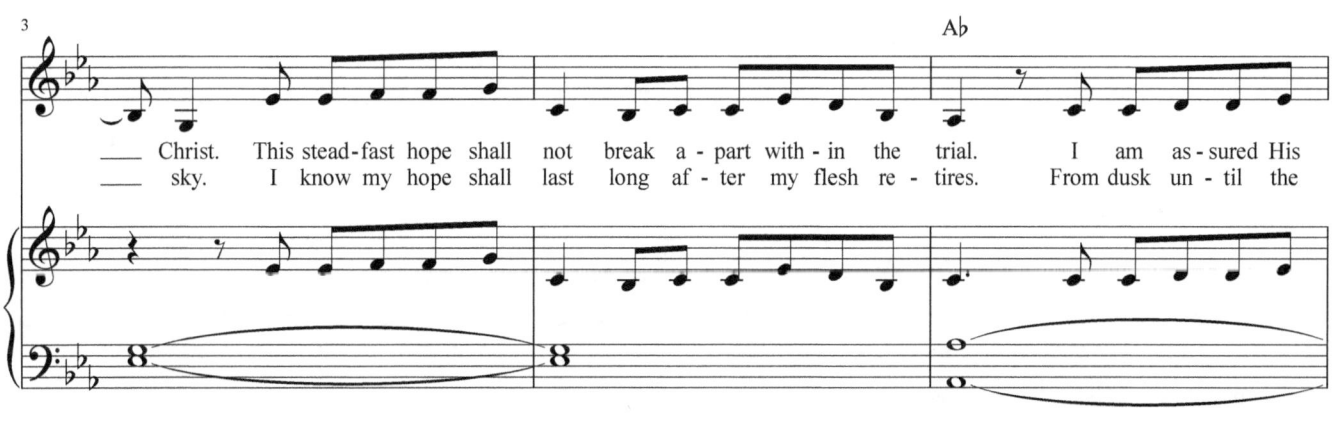

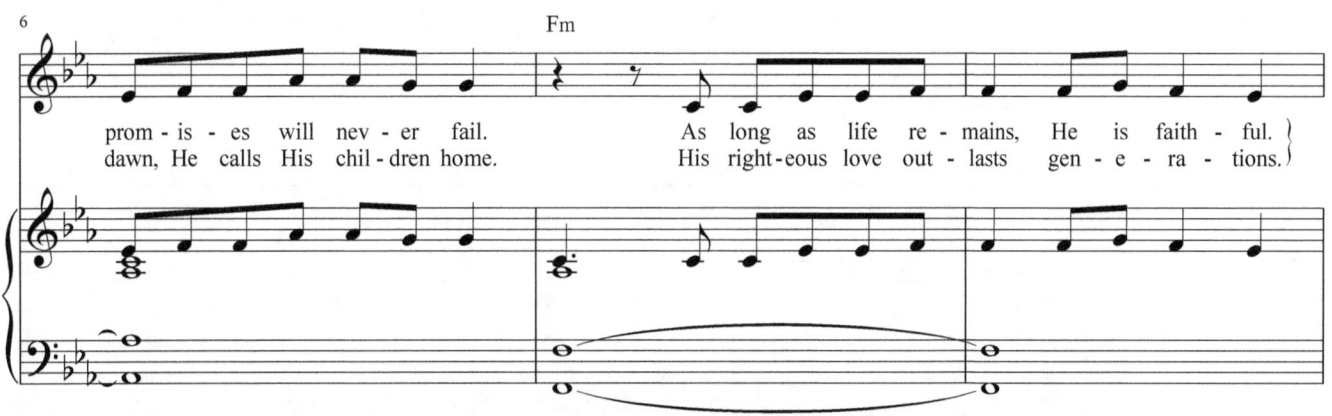

© 2016 Hillsong Music Publishing.
All rights reserved. International copyright secured. Used by permission.
Tel: +61 2 8853 5300 Email: publishing@hillsong.com CCLI Song No. 7069097

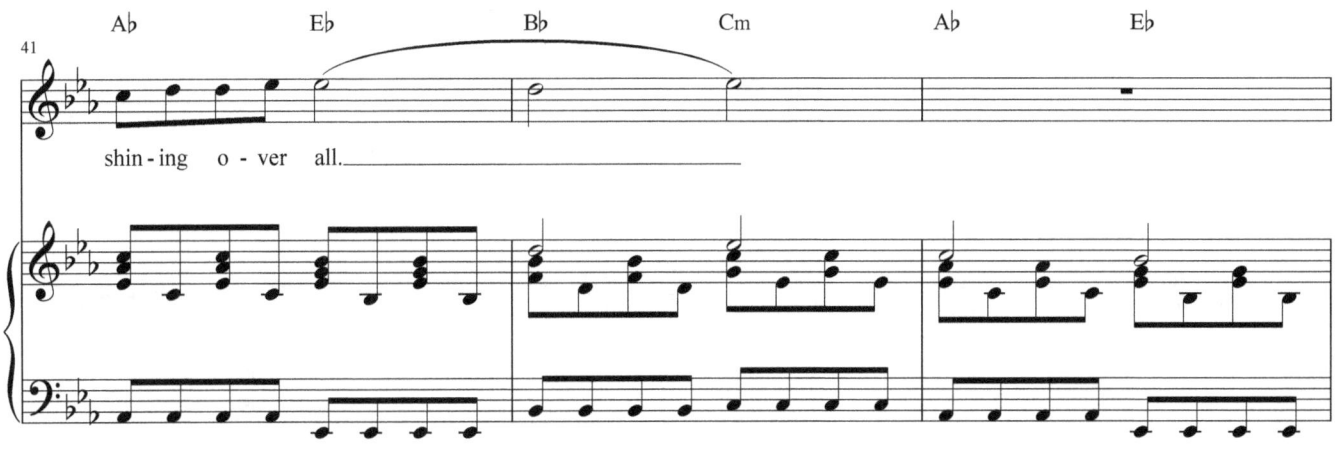
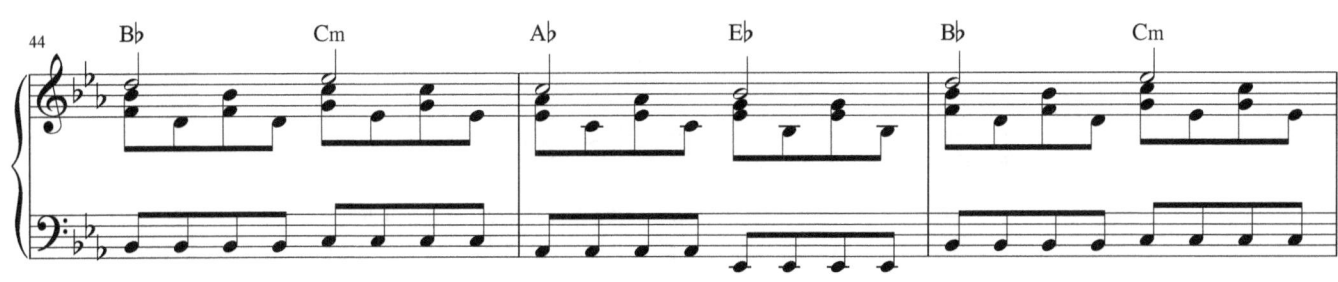
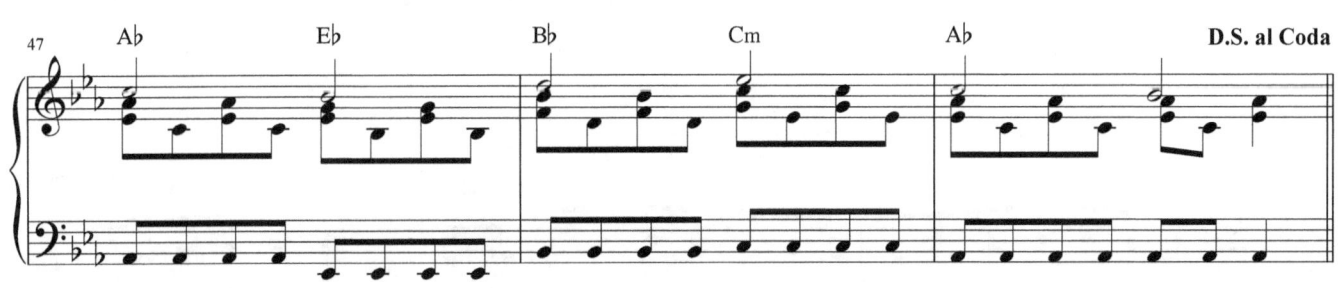

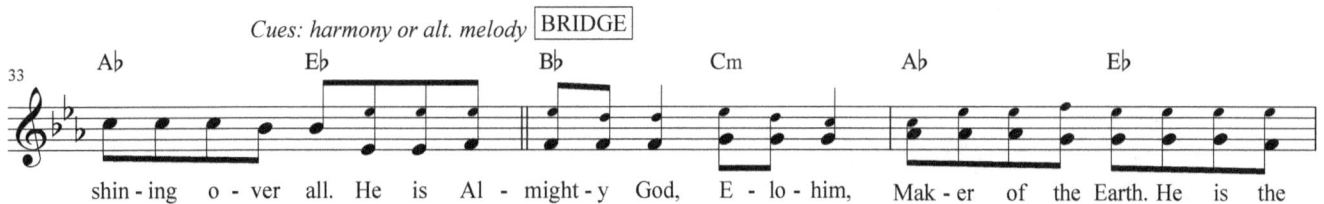
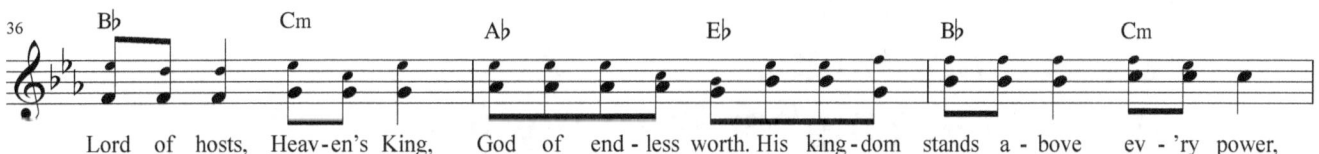

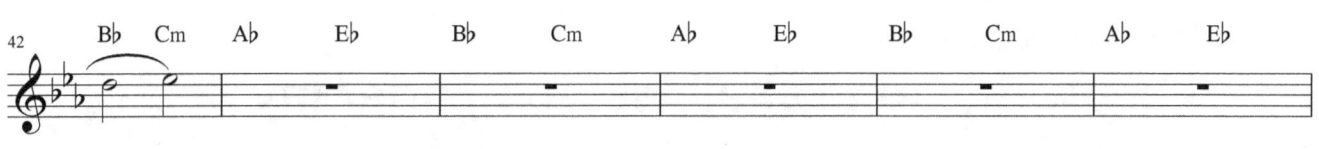
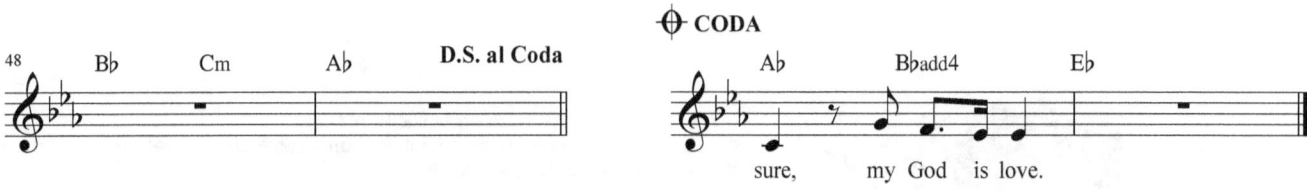

ELOHIM

Words and Music by Marty Sampson

VERSE 1:
I stand upon the solid rock of faith in Christ
This steadfast hope shall not break apart within the trial
I am assured
His promises will never fail
As long as life remains
He is faithful

CHORUS:
God is patient
God is kind
He does not envy
He does not boast
His ways are higher than my own
His thoughts consume the great unknown
Of this alone I am sure
My God is love

VERSE 2:
I draw my breath under His created windswept sky
I know my hope shall last long after my flesh retires

© 2016 Hillsong Music Publishing.
All rights reserved. International copyright secured.
Used by permission.
Tel: +61 2 8853 5300
Email: publishing@hillsong.com
CCLI Song No. 7069097

From dusk until the dawn He calls His children home
His righteous love outlasts generations

BRIDGE:
He is Almighty God
Elohim
Maker of the earth
He is the Lord of hosts
Heaven's King
God of endless worth
His kingdom stands above
Every power
Every living soul
His love is like the sun
Ever true
Shining over all

© 2016 Hillsong Music Publishing.
All rights reserved. International copyright secured.
Used by permission.
Tel: +61 2 8853 5300
Email: publishing@hillsong.com
CCLI Song No. 7069097

I WILL BOAST IN CHRIST

Words and Music by
SCOTT LIGERTWOOD & REUBEN MORGAN
Additional lyrics from "Nothing But The Blood" (Traditional)

© 2016 Hillsong Music Publishing.
All rights reserved. International copyright secured. Used by permission.
Tel: +61 2 8853 5300 Email: publishing@hillsong.com CCLI Song No. 7068427

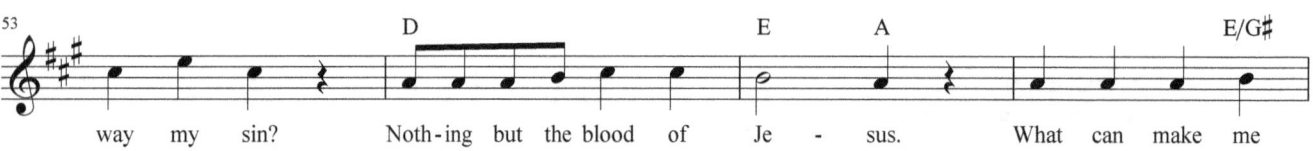
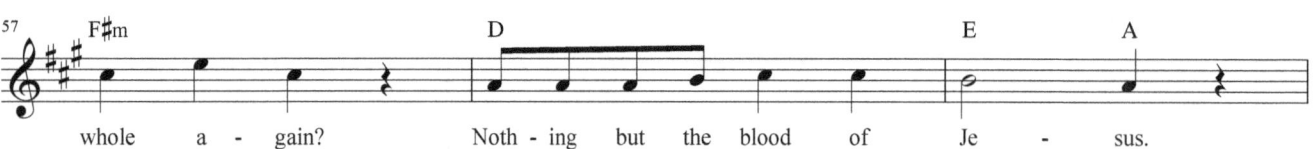
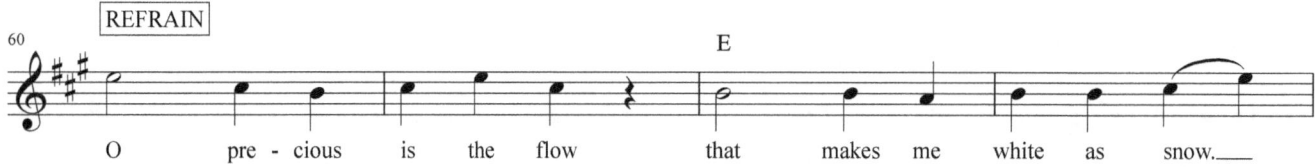

I WILL BOAST IN CHRIST

**Words and Music by
Scott Ligertwood & Reuben Morgan**
Additional lyrics from "Nothing But The Blood", Traditional

VERSE 1:
All I have because of Jesus
All this promise
Won for me
When He paid the highest ransom
Once for always
For my freedom

CHORUS:
I will boast in Christ alone
His righteousness
Not my own
I will cling to Christ my hope
His mercy reigns
Now and forever

VERSE 2:
Love will never lose its power
All my failures could not erase
Now I walk within Your favour
Grace unending
My salvation

© 2016 Hillsong Music Publishing.
All rights reserved. International copyright secured.
Used by permission.
Tel: +61 2 8853 5300
Email: publishing@hillsong.com
CCLI Song No. 7068427

BRIDGE:
What can wash away my sin
Nothing but the blood of Jesus
What can make me whole again
Nothing but the blood of Jesus

REFRAIN:
O precious is the flow
That makes me white as snow
No other fount I know
Nothing but the blood of Jesus

© 2016 Hillsong Music Publishing.
All rights reserved. International copyright secured.
Used by permission.
Tel: +61 2 8853 5300
Email: publishing@hillsong.com
CCLI Song No. 7068427

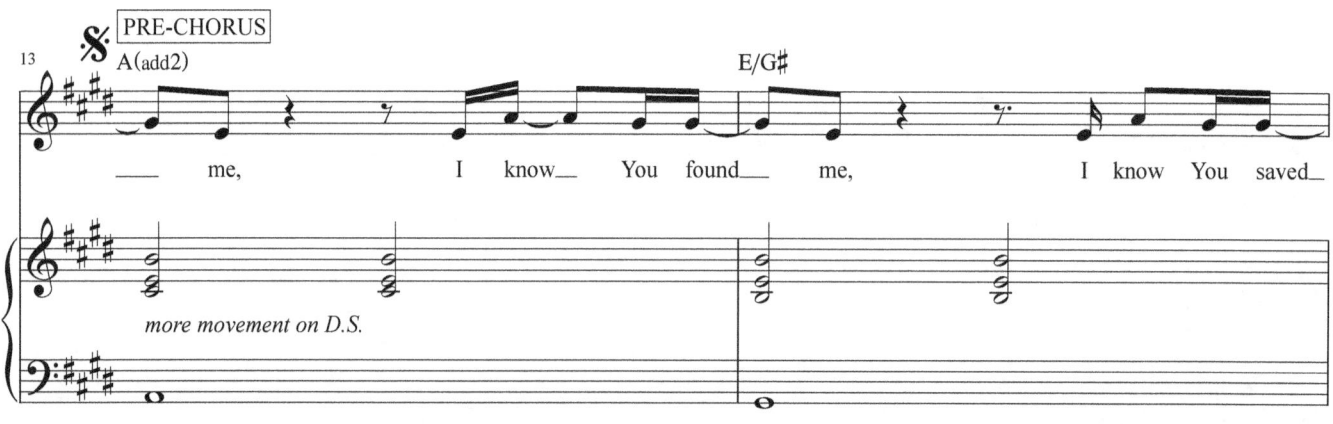

D.S. al Coda
C♯m7
E
E/G♯
- son walls_ can hold___ me, I will sing__ like I___ am free.__ 'Cause I know_ You love_
CODA
INSTRUMENTAL
Amaj7
F♯m7
E
C♯m7
A
B
C♯m

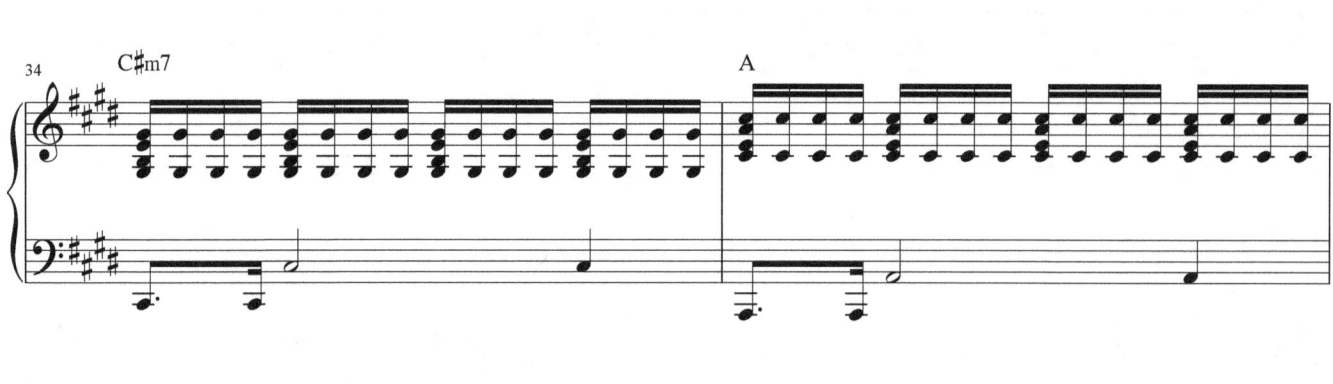

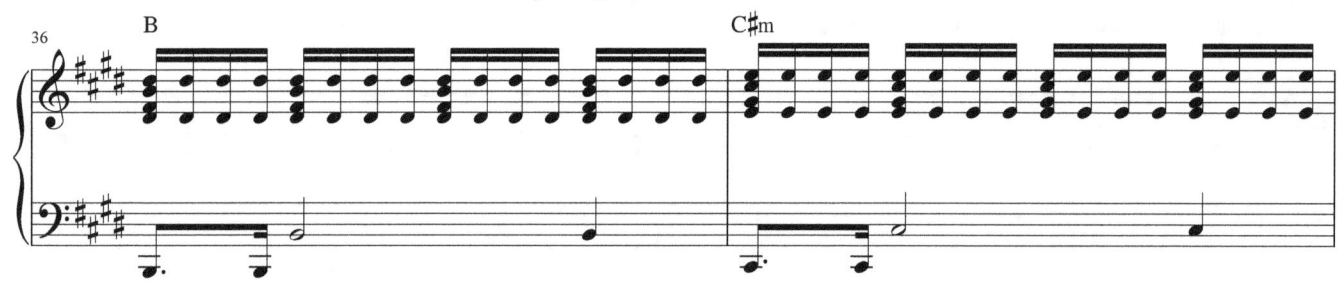

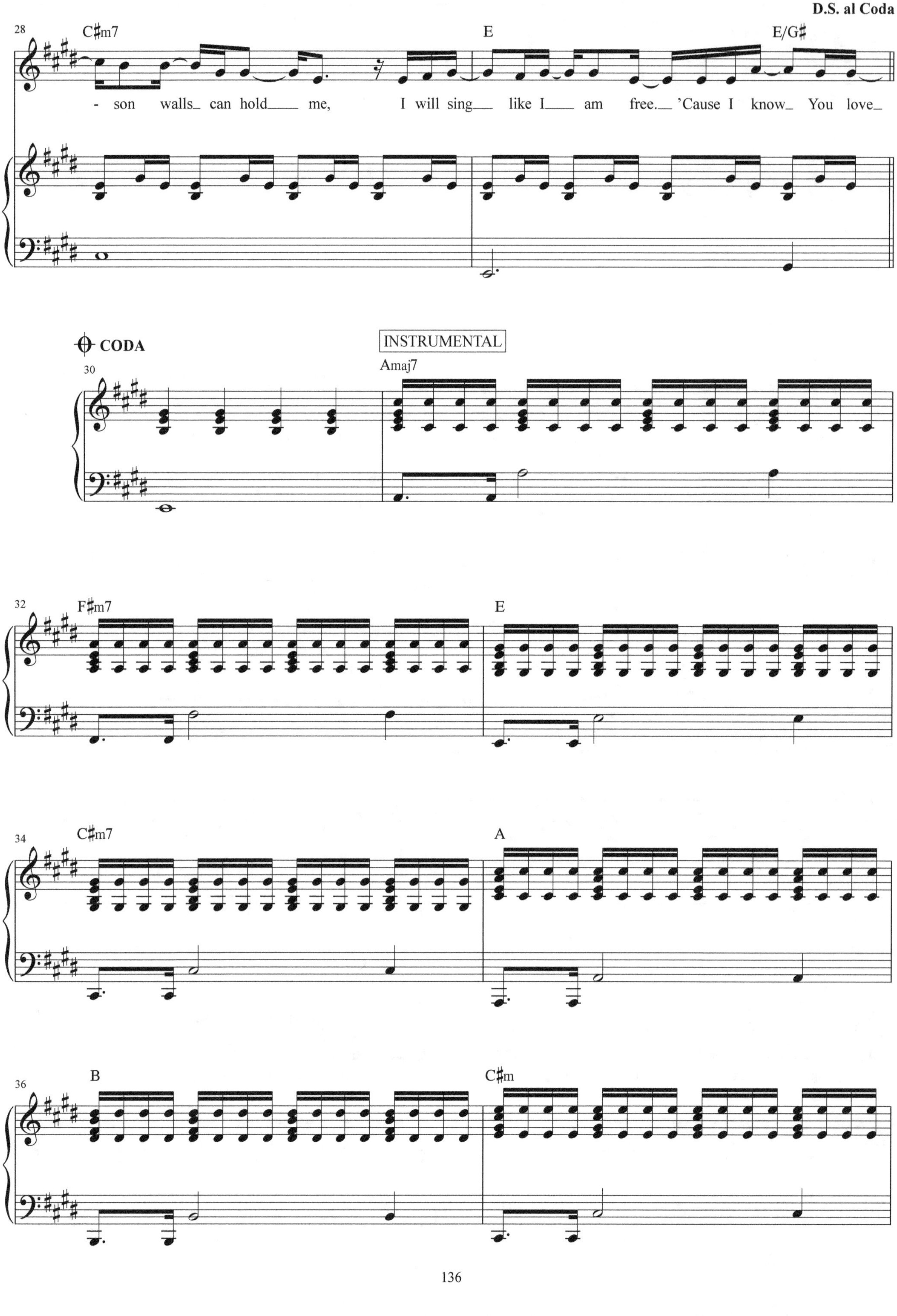

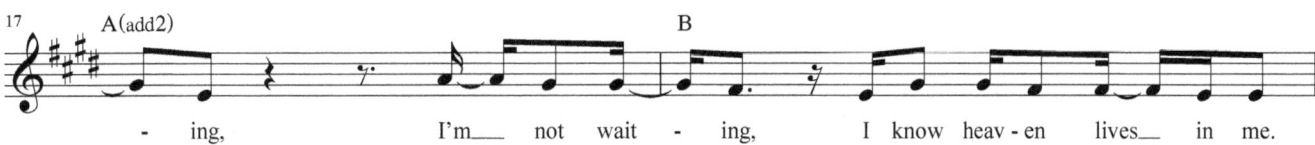
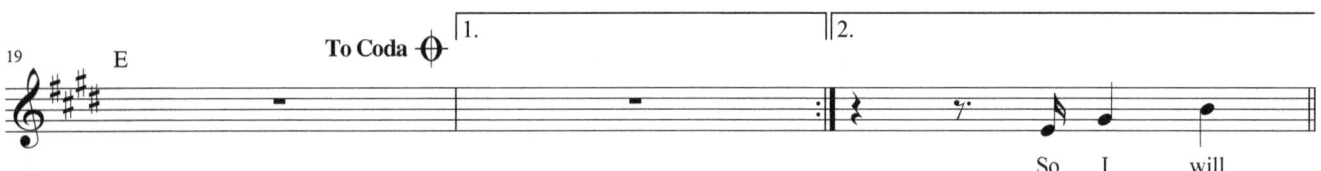

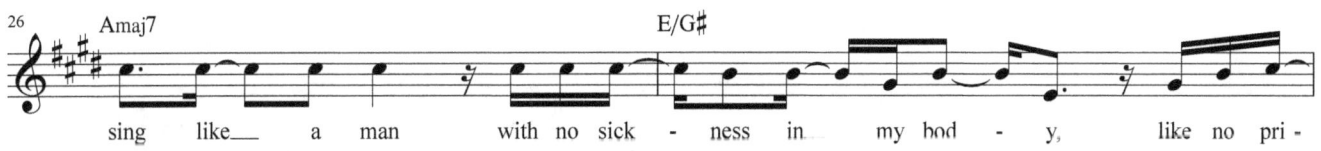

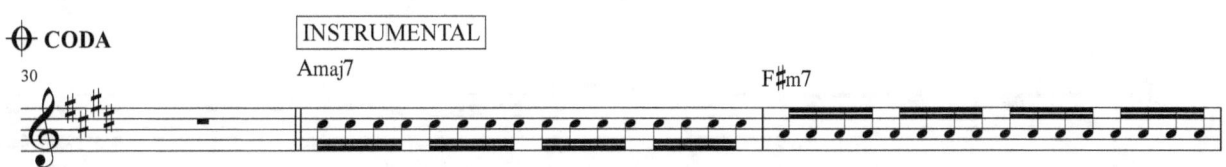

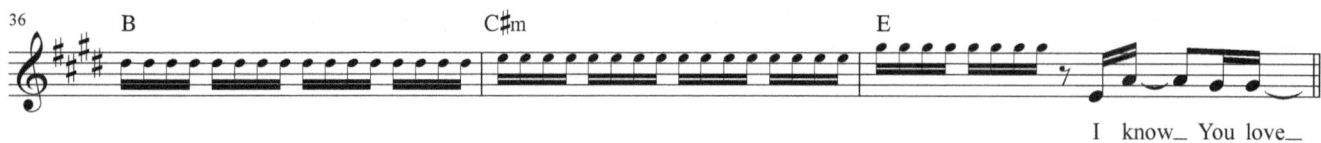

PRE-CHORUS
E A
like I am free. 'Cause I know You love me, I know You found
F♯m7 E
me, I know You saved me and Your grace will nev-er fail
C♯m7 A
me. And while I'm wait-ing, I'm not wait-
B E
ing, I know heav-en lives in me. I'll sing
BRIDGE
A F♯m7 E
ho-ly, ho-ly. My heart cries ho-
C♯m7 A B C♯m7
ly. As it is in heav-en, it is in me.
BRIDGE
E A B C♯m7
I'll sing ho-ly, ho-ly. My heart cries ho-
E A B E
ly. As it is in heav-en, it is in me.

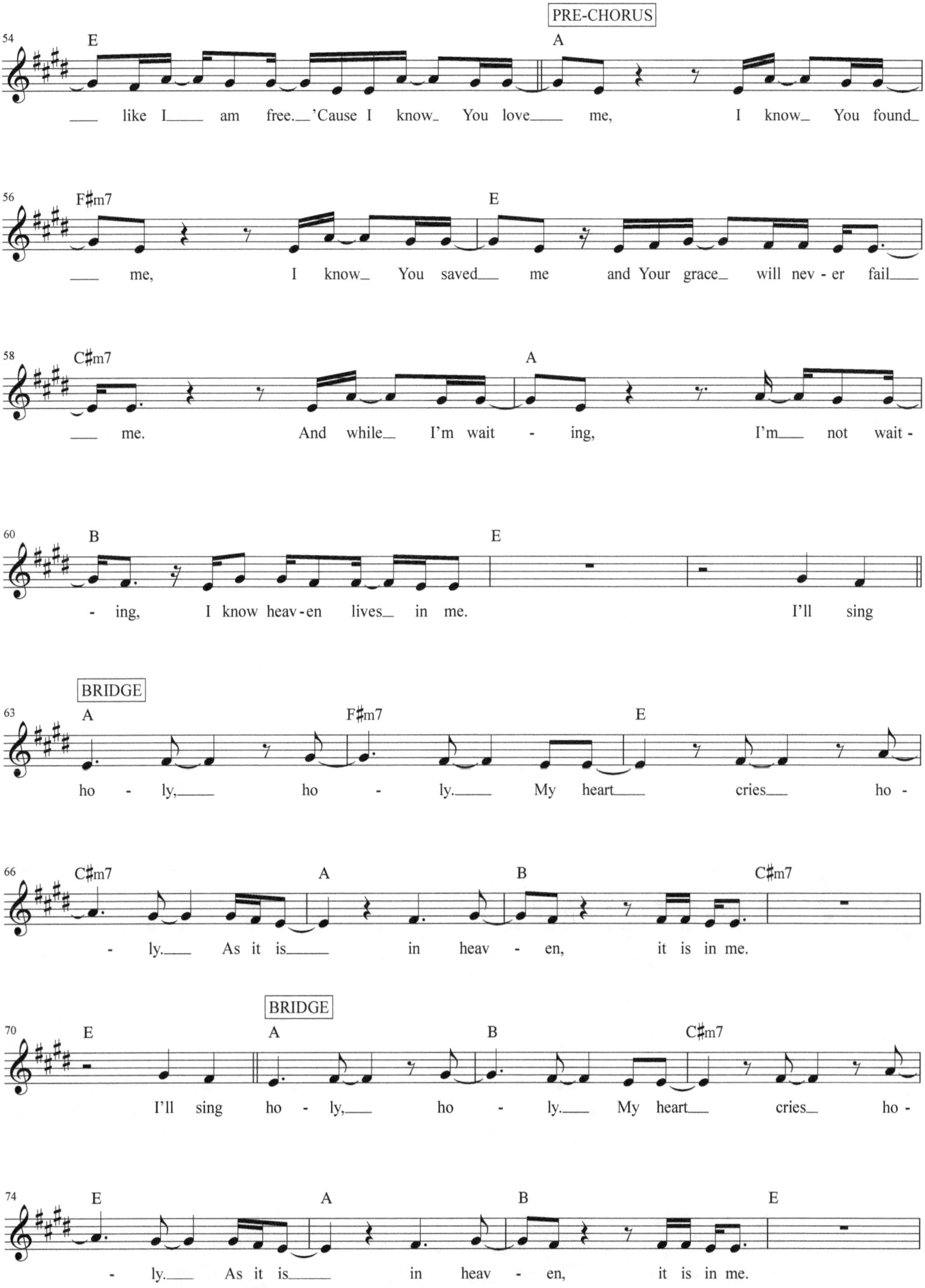

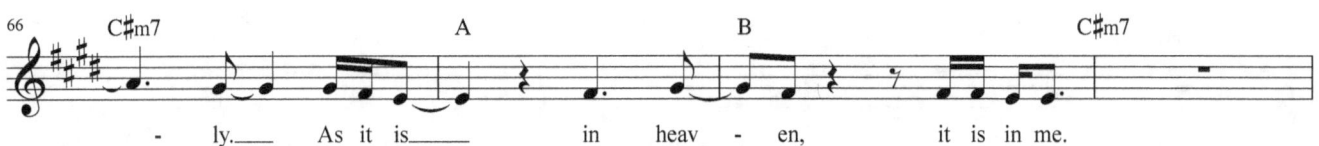

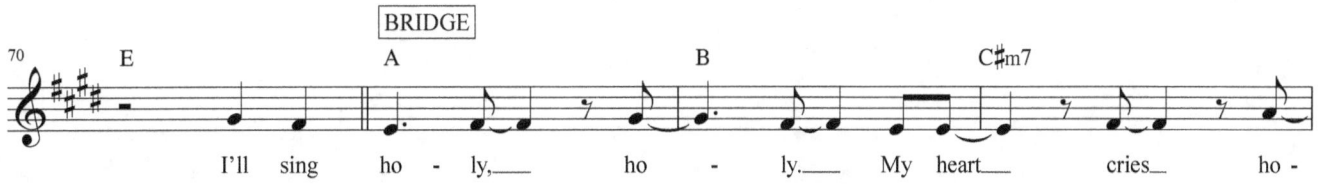

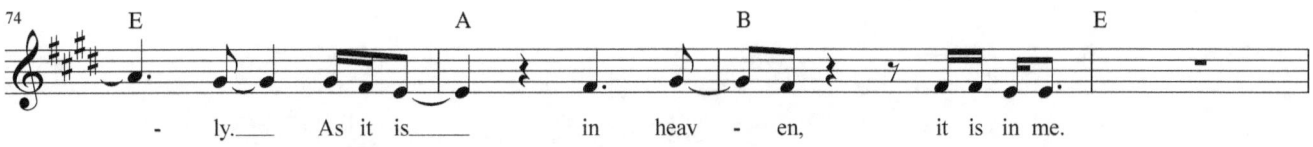

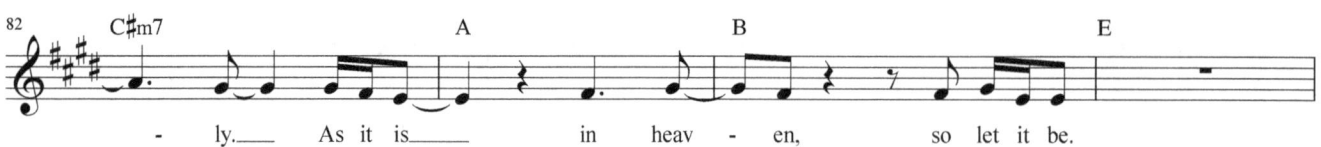

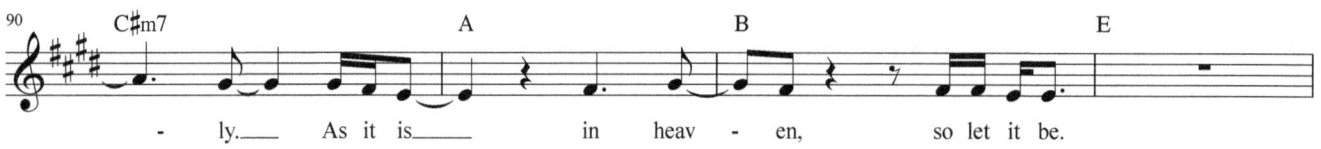
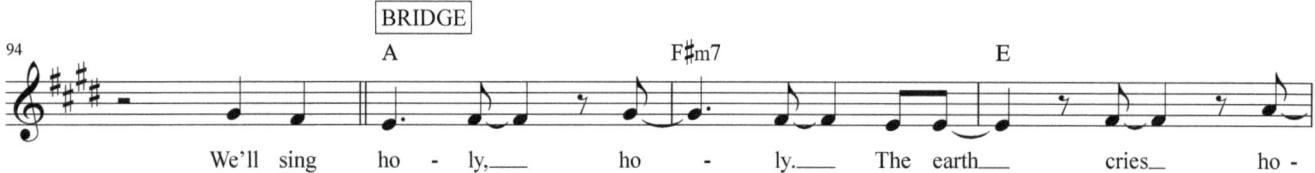
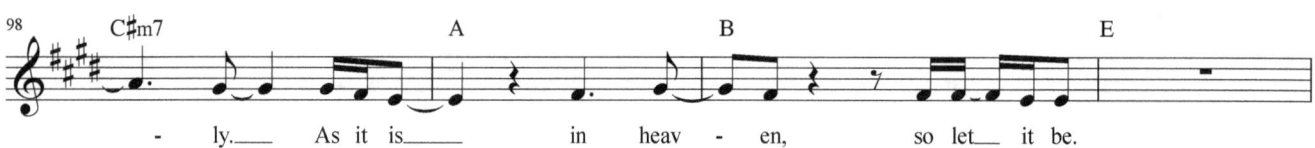
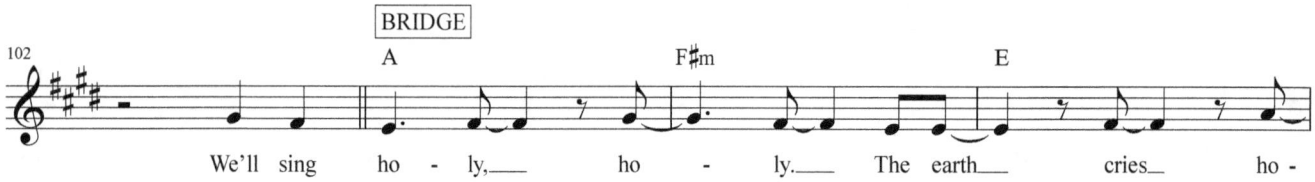

AS IT IS (IN HEAVEN)

**Words and Music by
Joel Houston & Ben Fielding**

VERSE 1:
**Whether now or then
Death is not my end
I know heaven waits for me
Though the road seems long
I'll never walk alone
I've got all I need to sing**

PRE-CHORUS:
**I know You love me
I know You found me
I know You saved me
And Your grace will never fail me
And while I'm waiting
I'm not waiting
I know heaven lives in me**

VERSE 2:
**Should I suffer long
This is not my home
I know heaven waits for me**

© 2016 Hillsong Music Publishing.
All rights reserved. International copyright secured.
Used by permission.
Tel: +61 2 8853 5300
Email: publishing@hillsong.com
CCLI Song No. 7068429

Though the night is dark
Heaven owns my heart
I've got all I need to sing

CHORUS:
So I will sing like I will there
In the fearless light of glory
Where the darkness cannot find me
And Your face is all I see
I will sing like a man
With no sickness in my body
Like no prison walls can hold me
I will sing like I am free

BRIDGE:
I'll sing holy holy
My heart cries holy
As it is in heaven
It is in me

We'll sing holy holy
The earth cries holy
As it is in heaven
So let it be